'ROUND NEWPORT

Recalling 60 Years of Jazz
'Round Newport, Rhode Island

By Burt Jagolinzer

'Round Newport

Recalling 60 Years of Jazz
'Round Newport, Rhode Island

By

Burt Jagolinzer

Visit our website **at www.StillwaterPress.com** for more information.

First Stillwater River Publications Edition

ISBN-10: 0-692-23153-6
ISBN-13:978-069223-153-1

Library of Congress Control Number: 2014942333

1 2 3 4 5 6 7 8 9 10
Written by Burt Jagolinzer
Cover design by Dawn M. Porter
Published by Stillwater River Publications, Glocester, RI, USA

Dedication

This book is dedicated to my love for:

My significant other, Nancy Parenti
My brother and his wife, Ken and Ruthie
My daughters, Cheryl and Wendy
My grandchildren, Caroline, Zach and Jacob

To the memories of:

My parents, Lilyan and Charles
My brother, Phil
And my friends, Bob Parenti, Clay Osborn, Annette Clayborn, Bill
Angel, Billy Weston, Gordon Sweeney, Brenda Lupino, Lucille
Armstrong, Dave Brubeck, Larry Wein and Joyce Wein

Table of Contents

Why, 'Round Newport?..i

Preface...iii

Introduction...v

Writing My Story...ix

1. The Early Years...1

2. Childhood...6

3. The First Festival...10

4. My Early Musical Years...19

5. The Second Festival and Changes...23

6. Rhode Island Jazz..35

7. Perpetuating the History of Jazz..51

8. Friday Evenings at the Casino..55

9. The 1956 Jazz Festival...58

10. My Friendship with Joyce Wein..62

11. The 1957 Newport Jazz Festival...64

12. The 1958 Newport Jazz Festival at Freebody Park.................67

13. Jazz, A Major Influence on Integration..................................72

14. The 1959 Newport Jazz Festival...74

15. U.S. Army & Music...76

16. Hitchhiking with Duke...79

17. The 1960 Newport Jazz Festival...82

18. The 1960 Newport Jazz Festival – Riot at the Festival............86

19. From U.S. Army to Greater Boston...90

20. A Long Walk with Jazz...92

21. An Attempt to Replace Jazz..94

22. The 1962 Newport Jazz Festival – Return to Newport............96

23. The 1963 Newport Jazz Festival...103

24. The Music Begins to Change..108

25. Accepting the Changing of Jazz...112

26. The 1964 Newport Jazz Festival – The Last at Freebody Park...114

27. The 1965 Newport Jazz Festival...116

28. Enjoying the Boston Jazz Scene...123

29. While Searching for Jazz in Boston.....................................127

30. The 1966 Newport Jazz Festival...130

31. The 1967 Newport Jazz Festival...136

32. Collecting Jazz Albums..142

33. The 1968 Newport Jazz Festival...144

34. The 1969 Newport Jazz Festival 146

35. Recognizing Jazz's Unusual Musical Sounds......................148

36. Quality Jazz in Arizona...151

37. Finding a New Life and Direction..155

38. The 1970 Newport Jazz Festival...157

39. The 1971 Newport Jazz Festival – The Second Riot..............162

40. The Festivals in New York City, Boston and Saratoga...........164

41. The New York City Years..166

42. The Special Voice of Johnny Hartman.................................169

43. The 1981 Newport Jazz Festival – The Return to Newport.......171

44. The 1982 Newport Jazz Festival...176

45. The 1983 Newport Jazz Festival...180

46. For the Love of Willie Love...184

47. The 1984 Newport Jazz Festival...186

48. Memorable Times with Dave McKenna.................................190

49. The 1985 Newport Jazz Festival...194

50. Sudhalter and Sherman...198

51. The 1986 Newport Jazz Festival...200

52. A Musician's Life in New York City....................................205

53. The 1987 Newport Jazz Festival..207

54. The 1988 Newport Jazz Festival..210

55. The 1989 Newport Jazz Festival..213

56. Dissecting a Few of the Greats...216

57. My Trumpet, on a CD..218

58. The 1990 Newport Jazz Festival..220

59. The 1991 Newport Jazz Festival..223

60. Jazz in Europe..225

61. The 1992 Newport Jazz Festival..227

62. Classical Jazz, At Its Best..229

63. The 1993 Newport Jazz Festival..231

64. The 1994 Newport Jazz Festival..233

65. The 1995 Newport Jazz Festival..236

66. The 1996 Newport Jazz Festival..239

67. Jazz Week in Newport...242

68. The 1997 Newport Jazz Festival..245

69. The 1998 Newport Jazz Festival..249

70. The 1999 Newport Jazz Festival..253

71. A Day and a Half with Harry Connick, Jr...................................256

72. The 2000 Newport Jazz Festival..258

73. Re-Discovering Mike Renzi...264

74. The 2001 Newport Jazz Festival..268

75. The 2002 Newport Jazz Festival..273

76. Two Days with Tony Bennett...277

77. The 2003 Newport Jazz Festival..281

78. The 2004 Newport Jazz Festival..284

79. The 2005 Newport Jazz Festival..290

80. The 2006 Newport Jazz Festival..295

81. The Providence Union's Effort in Jazz..................................298
82. The 2007 Newport Jazz Festival..300
83. Playing Piano at the Tavern on the Green..........................305
84. The 2008 Newport Jazz Festival..307
85. The 2009 Newport Jazz Festival..311
86. The 2010 Newport Jazz Festival..314
87. Old Musicians Attempt Coming Back................................320
88. The 2011 Newport Jazz Festival..322
89. The 2012 Newport Jazz Festival..326
90. A Jazz Find in Canada..331
91. The 2013 Newport Jazz Festival..333
92. Today and the Future of Jazz..337
93. Passing the Torch..339
Appendix I - The So-Called Nick-Names..............................341
Appendix II - The Author's Choice..342
'Round Newport Lyrics..347
Acknowledgements..349
Photo Credits..350

Why, *'Round Newport?*

The late, great pianist and composer Thelonious Monk wrote one of early jazz's most successful tunes, titled *'Round Midnight*.

It became so popular in the jazz world, that many musicians to-day perform the composition as part of their regular repertoire.

Monk's world came to life *'Round* Midnight, whereas my world came to life *'Round* Newport, Rhode Island, thus, the name of my book.

I have also written the lyrics and music for a song titled *'Round Newport*, the lyrics of which are printed at the end of this book. I expect the song to be released in a few months.

Preface

Very little research has gone into the writing of this work. My own collection of original programs from the Newport, Rhode Island festivals helped me recall many of the outstanding performances and incidents that took place over the years.

George Wein's excellent book, *Myself Among Others*, (written with Nate Chinen) documents his views as a producer of the festivals, whereas my book is written as an observer, delivered from the perspective of a paying customer.

As a jazz enthusiast, a former musician and a lover of the arts, I approached this writing with the full intention of being honest and fair in my evaluation and recollection of the people and incidents that occurred before me.

Some sixty years of attending the Newport, Rhode Island festivals and my own life experiences with music form the basis for most of the information presented here.

Introduction

I have in my possession most of the original programs from nearly sixty years of jazz festival performances at Newport, Rhode Island.

These booklets list numerous jazz giants, many who performed when they were not yet well-known or had not yet reached their peak. The festivals deserve much of the credit for the professional advancements they made shortly after their gigs on the Newport stage. This exposure gave them the chance for popularity around the world.

Many of these successful artists have claimed that once they finished performing in Newport, they had finally, "made it to the top."

President Bill Clinton, while visiting Newport during his second election campaign, said that while growing up in Arkansas and playing the saxophone, he hoped to perform someday on the stage at a Newport, Rhode Island festival.

Even today, the Newport jazz stage is considered the finest place for both music veterans and new musicians alike. The annual Newport Jazz Festival has been called "the mother of all jazz festivals" by many critics. These performers still get a boost to their careers from having played at Newport.

The reflections presented in this book document the importance and successes of the performances, from the beginning of the Newport Rhode Island Jazz Festivals in 1954 through the changes and growth of the art form today.

This book represents my own descriptions and opinions of these annual events woven around experiences of my own life in music.

'Round Newport is filled with my meetings and interactions with many famous individuals, both current and deceased, connected to early and contemporary jazz.

I was interviewed by National Public Radio (NPR) in February of 2001 by reporter Greg Fitzgerald. NPR was very interested in my take on the early festivals in Newport and my interplay with key people from that era. Greg spent several hours in Newport's

Hotel Viking recording my comments, which were later replayed on Nancy Wilson's weekly NPR program.

Many of my friends and relatives heard and enjoyed these various interviews and recognized that I had something unique to contribute to jazz history.

Later, local cable television chased me for interviews for their own jazz shows, such as the program hosted by Stan Kenton authority, Tony Agostinelli. I told several stories from the early festivals and from some of the special performances connected to those festivals.

The University of Rhode Island radio station WRIU also requested my presence, where I talked on several of their afternoon jazz studio shows with the late Bill Pandozzi.

In addition, I taught jazz history as an elective at The University of Rhode Island and at Salve Regina University back in the late 1980's.

Writing My Story

Jazz is made up of many rhythms, sounds, reactions and ex-pressions. While that mixture includes early African emotions and religious connections, it is truly one's own choice as to how to enjoy it best.

I had been weaned on early melodies with varied rhythms per-formed by a variety of different musicians, including the big bands of those days.

The music featured basic improvisations. It was a joy.

Individuals like Louis Armstrong learned how to use his horn to imitate the many instruments in a typical orchestra. His early recordings demonstrate his talent and effort. Armstrong also explored playing between the composer's melodies with previ-ously unheard improvisations.

Armstrong's achievements gave permission, so to speak, for other musicians to attempt these improvisations, and even more. This musical movement carried beautiful melodies, sometimes sweet and catchy, that were truly emotional and upbeat.

Most of these melodies were easy to remember, pleasing to the ear, and were easily identified with a talented performer or a specific studio recording artist.

But by the late 1960's the music began changing. The melodies became hidden.

Improvisation overtook many of the composer's themes and melodic objectives. It was the beginning of a new approach to jazz, challenging a period of music that lasted the previous six decades.

While these changes were taking place many of us had difficulty understanding, appreciating and even accepting the new style.

I have come to accept it -- but with reservations.

The early music concept that I had enjoyed had gone backstage. And as years passed, it became more difficult to find this older concept in the festival's programming. In its place was the new music that included the clashing of instruments with fusions of sounds and rhythms.

Some of my colleagues claimed the new style to be inspired by the performers' reactions to drugs, and the influence of world troubles.

Since the newer style was generally loud and different, it easily attracted the youth who had now become the majority ticket purchasers at the festivals.

Although I continue to attend these current festivals, and find enjoyment in the performances, it is the memories of those early festivals that I have chosen to write mostly about.

This newer music is better defined and reported by others who seem to enjoy the more modern concept.

And so this book is centered mostly around those concerts that occurred prior to the change. They are indelible recollections of the festivals' beginnings, many important historical events, interwoven with the personal experiences of my earliest discoveries in jazz.

Chapter 1
The Early Years

I was sitting next to Lucille Armstrong, Louis' special lady, when Billie Holiday came back to her seat.

Billie was carrying two colas. She gave one to a little girl who was sitting three seats away from her. Then she turned around and tapped me on the shoulder and asked, "Maybe you could enjoy this drink…young fella?" And she leaned forward to put the cup into my hands.

That day, I accepted a drink from the hands of the infamous Billie Holiday, a moment that some sixty years later remains truly special in my jazz-infected life.

'Round Newport

My closest friends and relatives have been encouraging me to put that story down on paper, as well as the many others that have taken place over my long romance with jazz. These pages are an attempt to share some of those stories with you.

This moment with Billie Holiday occurred during the very first Newport Jazz Festival in 1954 at The Casino on Newport's famed Bellevue Avenue.

The Casino is a special wooden structure that was built around the turn of the Twentieth Century as a tennis club and social center for Newport's upper class citizens. A part of it resembled the famous Wimbledon architecture of London, and the International Tennis Hall of Fame was established in an adjoining building at this site just months later.

Louis and Elaine Lorillard had planned the framework of this unique festival. Louis had served on the board of directors of The Casino.

In conversation, Elaine had always told me that she believed jazz musicians should perform on stage where total focus could give the audience the opportunity to enjoy their real talents.

She explained, "Jazz players were only available in dim-lit smoky night clubs or lounges, often very noisy. The talent was pushed into the worst corner of the establishment. We, the true jazz listeners, were being cheated. What a shame. I decided to do something about it."

She was to find out later that the musicians themselves, who began performing on stage, not only appreciated the opportunity to hear their fellow performers, but also the opportunity to come together and jam.

Even a novice like myself could see how these jams could bring these talents together, and the possible changes that could take place because of them.

As a result of the festival, many of the musicians would merge their talents. Some even formed new, spectacular groups. They also learned new ideas and improvements from their peers during this brand-new, unique exposure concept that Elaine had developed.

Elaine convinced her husband, who had been connected to the tobacco and travel industries, to put up the money to fund the first festival. Being a dear close friend, she confided in me about the problems she had organizing and producing the festival that first year.

Elaine, herself a credible singer and pianist, had wanted to hire John Hammond, a leading New York City producer and critic, but he was not available to lead the program. Next on her list was the recording guru (and jazz promoter) Norman Granz who chose not to get involved. Third on her list was Boston jazz club owner, George Wein.

George was excited by the offer. He had always wanted to put together a Tanglewood-type program for jazz, and he saw this as the opportunity to do it. "Without reservations, George began planning our first event."

Though the first festival was a great social success, it ended deep in the red. They tried again a year later, also without financial success, and the Lorillards talked about giving it up.

Although they had put up the financing, it was George who had truly created the program, put it together, and saw to its quick musical success.

To his credit, George Wein would later go out on his own to find sponsors, pick up the pieces, and continue the event. And for sixty years now, George has managed to keep it going, not only in Newport, but expanding to additional festivals in key locations around the world.

George Wein truly deserves the credit because of his personal dedication, commitment and love for this special art form. At the time, no one, including George, would have believed that he was to become the leading jazz promoter in the world.

We, the jazz music fans, musicians, agents, families, sponsors and the huge numbers of connected businesses, owe George our gratitude and more. How lucky we have been to have had this man spearhead the promotion, the expansion and the groundwork for the future of our unique music.

And little did I know that I would become the only person, it is believed, to have attended all the Newport jazz annual gatherings, both in Newport, Rhode Island and the stints in New York City.

Three years ago my friend, Gordon Sweeney, passed away. He and I had been to them all. Now I stand alone... except of course for George Wein, the producer.

Chapter 2
Childhood

I was raised in Providence, the capital city of tiny Rhode Island.

My dad played some violin.

My mom was a pianist, who as a youngster, was employed by some five theatres in downtown Providence playing the emotional background music for the silent movies of her day.

Mom stated openly, "I got paid one dollar for the entire week including matinees. I gave fifty-cents to my parents and I had enough left over to take five or six of my friends for ice-cream sundaes, which were two-cents each at the time. The remaining eighteen cents, I banked."

Burt Jagolinzer

I was the baby of the family with three brothers. Ken, the oldest dabbled with several instruments. Phil, the next oldest and I took piano lessons.

At age eleven I switched from piano to trumpet and began a true love for music at all levels. By high school I had played trombone, tuba and baritone horn.

My trumpet teacher, Henry Shapiro, was a lead horn player with the Rhode Island Philharmonic Orchestra. He booked me on a local radio station (WPAW, Pawtucket) in a popular weekly amateur entertainment show called *Leave it to Youth.*

On the show, I played the tune *Cruising Down the River* and won a twenty-five dollar gift certificate to a local department store. My mom bought me a new baseball cap and a pair of pants with the money.

Around this time my brothers and I befriended a local popular disc jockey named Marc Sheila, who had been working at radio station WPAW and whose theme song was Harry James' *Opus Number One*. His regular daily show featured some great jazz and many big-band specials.

I continued with my lessons and struggled with triple and double tonguing. I would continually mess up playing *Flight of the Bumble-Bee* which at the time was considered the triumph of cornet playing. But my tone was soft and sweet, and my teacher (and band leader), thought I had a good future in music. I even learned my cornet playing could be a formidable way to earn spending money, that I surely needed at the time.

But the real fun was performing with terrific and gifted musicians, which made the hard work worthwhile. Many became longtime friends.

My introduction to real jazz was in 1948. I had just turned nine years-old. Ken, my oldest brother was almost seventeen. He took me to the famous Celebrity Club, at Randall Square on the corner of North Main Street in Providence.

It was a Sunday afternoon, and we caught the final singing performance of the great Joe Williams. Ken had to pay two dollars to enter the back door. There was no charge for me.

We were only allowed to stand in the back without drinks. The club served alcohol and you had to be 21 to drink. Behind us at the top of the stairs were a series of private rooms reserved for the "star" entertainers.

Out of one particular room came The Will Mastin Trio which starred Sammy Davis, Jr.

Sammy was dressed in a black suit and tie with white shirt and brown and white tap shoes. As Sammy strolled by us he took notice of me, being the youngest in the place, put his arm around me and said, *"Hope you enjoy our gig, kid."*

I did, and Sammy stole the show. He sang with his loud and gifted voice, danced and tapped like Mr. Bojangles, and imitated Jimmy Durante, Bing Crosby, Frank Sinatra and Liberace.

Sammy wisely paid special respect to his father and uncle, the other two members of the trio, not wanting to accept complete credit for the performance.

I was totally taken by Sammy, his talent, and the audience response that came with him.

A few weeks later, Ken and I returned to the Celebrity Club to enjoy the music of Billy Eckstine featuring a new young gal singer named Sarah Vaughan.

I won't forget Sarah's clear and talented voice nor the deep unusual voice of Billy Eckstine.

Little did I know what these early visits to that club were to mean to me, and the effect they would have on what was to follow.

Chapter 3
The First Festival

The first Newport Jazz Festival was held on Saturday evening, July 17, 1954.

I was just fourteen years-old and my friend, Barry Alperin, and I had been planning to attend this special jazz gathering.

At that time we were both members of the Sayles Junior High School Marching Band in Pawtucket. I played trumpet and Barry played clarinet.

Barry's mother drove us to The Casino in Newport with tickets in one hand, and a bag of red pistachios in the other.

First Newport Jazz Festival Program, 1954

We arrived a few minutes early for the event. We were to do the same on Sunday as well. My family was to return us after the events.

Most attendees were dressed in the night club fashion of the day, gentlemen in jackets with ties, ladies attired in gowns, colorful sun dresses and high heels. It was a lovely scene not expected at a jazz setting.

Both Barry and I, dressed neatly in sporty clothes, felt a bit uncomfortable.

Our seats were excellent in the fourth row, right-center.

The lady sitting on my right turned out to be Lucille Armstrong the wife of Louis Armstrong. She had come without Louis who had had a gig in a club in Harlem that weekend. She and two ladies seated to her right had decided to come on their own, curious to see what this concert would bring to the struggling art form.

The printed program which is still in my possession, listed a scattering of vocalists, instrumentals, a couple of quartets, one quintet and a trio.

The Master of Ceremonies was to be Stan Kenton, the noted teacher, composer, bandleader and longtime jazz enthusiast.

Although I had heard Kenton on the radio and on records, and had recognized his unique approach to jazz, it was meeting him and his musicians in person, way back in 1954, that became an indelible memory.

Some individuals compared Kenton's sound and music to that of the Glen Miller Orchestra. But I went the other way, thinking his genius in rhythm and sound to be totally different, giving permission to other musicians seeking new directions in jazz.

To this day I believe that Stan Kenton's influence is truly an important achievement often forgotten in the history of the jazz art form. I feel that jazz musical students today should be obliged to study the work of Stan Kenton.

The evening's program exploded with the first of two jam sessions, one early in the schedule, the other at the very end of the event. Today, it is hard to imagine these great names all coming together on one stage.

The list included the trumpets of Dizzy Gillespie, Wild Bill Davidson, and Bobby Hackett, the clarinets of Pee Wee Russell and Peanuts Hucko, the trombone of Vic Dickenson, Herb Ellis on guitar, Milt Jackson on vibes, the young Gerry Mulligan on baritone-sax, Ray Brown on bass and Oscar Peterson on piano. It was a very special happening. People were dancing in the aisles.

Although the jam sessions stole the show, I must not overlook the vocal performances of Lee Wiley and Billie Holiday.

Billie and the great saxophonist Lester Young had made many recordings together in earlier days, but they had not been talking to each other for years. Many people had tried to bring them back together, but to no avail.

That evening, Lester walked out on stage and reunited the famous couple.

He began his accompaniment when she opened with *Billie's Blues*. It was a gas.

To this day I have never heard *St. James Infirmary* sung by anyone even close to the way Billie performed it that evening. I had tears in my eyes throughout.

She was certainly at the peak of her career that evening. Tragically, she was to begin a downhill slide a short time later.

♫ ♫ ♫

The Sunday performance was indeed different.

The afternoon scheduled a Jazz Forum at 4 p.m. Father Norman O'Connor was the moderator of a panel consisting of Henry Cowell of the Peabody Institute, Professor Marshall Stearns of Hunter College and Willis Janis of Spelman College.

I was disappointed in the forum, as they tried to justify jazz's place in culture. Like many of us, I knew that jazz needed no justification at all. Jazz was truly an American art form to be fitted easily into the existing culture of this country...and beyond. Yet, I attended the forum, and even said a few words, sharing my feelings with the panel.

Unfortunately, the rain threatened to tarnish the evening performance. Not being prepared for the weather we covered ourselves with whatever plastic we could find. We still got soaked. But true jazz fans knew that the show would go on.

The evening's performances included a musical collage intended to be a tribute to Count Basie. It featured the great Lester Young on tenor, Buck Clayton on trumpet, Vic Dickenson on bone, Jo Jones on drums, Milt Hinton on bass and the magnificent Teddy Wilson on piano.

They played all the spectacular numbers made famous by Bill Basie and his orchestra. It was wonderful.

Following that thriller came the Oscar Peterson Trio with Ray Brown on bass and Herb Ellis on electric guitar.

Peterson's freedom on the piano was his own development. He used his classical background, skillfully integrated with his magic touch, to be different from other great jazz pianists.

Pee Wee Russell

It was a terrific choice that helped balance the loud group that had just performed.

Next up was Dizzy's Quintet, with Wade Legge on piano, Charlie Persip on drums, Lou Hackney on bass and featuring Hank Mobley on sax.

Dizzy's cheeks and horn drew the crowd's attention. The group was upbeat and very casual as it captured new improvisations that many of us had not previously heard.

The final performance from the first half of the show fronted The George Shearing Quintet, featuring George Devens on vibes.

I had already seen Shearing at George Wein's jazz club, Storyville, in Boston just a few weeks before. His performance here was just as good, and the crowd loved it.

After intermission, the Erroll Garner Trio took the stage with Jo Jones on drums and Milt Hinton on bass.

The crowd responded well to Erroll's own rhythm and grunts ending with original ballads and arrangements that separated him from the other great pianists of the day.

After Erroll Garner came Lennie Tristano on piano with Lee Konitz on sax. Supporting them was Billy Bauer on guitar, Peter Ind on bass and Jeff Morton on drums.

Next to perform was the great Gene Krupa Trio featuring Gene on the solo sticks, with Teddy Napoleon at piano and Eddie Shu on tenor.

We all loved Krupa's long arrangements but his dynamite solos brought us to our feet.

Finally, Ella Fitzgerald took the stage with John Lewis at the piano, Jimmy Woode at bass, and Shadow Wilson on drums.

Ella stole the show. She was near the peak of her long and extended career, and the crowd rose, humming and cheering her invigorating performance. I was in heaven.

To top off the evening, and the first festival, was the ending jam session.

Stan Kenton was featured at the piano, and most of the artists returned to the stage and rambled through several pieces that truly represented the uniqueness of this special happening.

That first festival had ended as a positive social and musical success. It didn't take me too long to realize that I had been to a ground-breaking and historic event, all for the love of jazz.

My dad was waiting for us at the end of the evening. We couldn't wait to tell him and our friends about our terrific evening and about the amazing performances we had just experienced.

Chapter 4
My Early Musical Years

It was my talent with the baritone horn that gave me the opportunity to perform in the Rhode Island Junior Philharmonic Orchestra, under the baton of the noted musician and director, Joseph Conte.

We performed at Symphony Hall in Boston, Tanglewood in Lennox, Massachusetts and Carnegie Hall in New York City, among other locations.

Though classical music and pop had been all around me, it was jazz that held my real interest. The rhythm, the enthusiasm, the joy, the freedom of improvisation and the unorthodox skills of these gifted jazz musicians stood out clearly before me. I was truly hooked.

'Round Newport

I was fifteen when I had read in the local tabloid that an English blind, jazz pianist had come across the Atlantic Ocean to perform at George Wein's Boston jazz nightclub, Storyville. His name was George Shearing and I had already read much about him.

Determined to see and hear him in person I got special permission from my Mom to take the train from Providence all the way to Boston.

I found my way to Storyville. Waiting at the lounge door was a large imposing gentleman. (I later discovered that his name was Larry Wein, older brother to George, the owner of that special jazz club). Larry wouldn't let me in. I was underage and could not be admitted to an alcohol-drinking setting.

I was humiliated and pleaded with him to let me stand in the back just to watch and listen to this special attraction. He said that he couldn't accommodate me. I told him that I had come by train from Providence just to take in the event and that I was not a drinker, nor had I any intention to drink alcohol. He said, "come back, kid in about an hour...and I'll see what I can do."

I returned in forty-minutes, and he graciously let me in to stand in the back. And he even bought me a ginger-ale.

I was thrilled and forever thankful to Larry Wein for that kind favor. Little did I know that I was to meet Larry at future Newport Festivals, and we became good friends.

Over the course of our friendship, Larry introduced me to many notable people, including University Chaplin Father Norman O'Connor, the jazz priest from Boston University, who was a long-time participant and friend of George and Joyce Wein.

Father O'Connor was to play important roles throughout the early festivals, acting as Master of Ceremonies during several concerts, addressing seminars and serving as George's advisor on many delicate issues.

On another occasion, Larry introduced me to the great Dave Brubeck, with whom we were to share lunch in 1955 at Gary's Handy Lunch on Lower Thames Street in Newport.

I remember Brubeck didn't like his ham and cheese sandwich served with too much mayo. Larry and I pigged-out with two hotdogs a piece.

Dave Brubeck was anxious to talk about his family and newly born son. He told us that they had chosen his son's name to be Darius after his famous music composition instructor, Darius Milhaud, from Mills College in Oakland, California. He told us that he hoped that his children would take to music and enjoy it as he did. But like many fathers, he said that whatever his son decided, would really be good enough for him and his wife.

Neither Larry nor I could have guessed of the future successes about to come to that whole family.

It was shortly after this lunch I was informed that Larry had passed away.

Today, I reflect on my friendship with Larry Wein. He was a soft, gentle man with a special love for his brother, music and people. I won't forget his firm handshake or his enthusiasm.

Chapter 5
The Second Festival and Changes

It was several weeks later, at the end of that summer, that I decided to help form a jazz quartet, *The Downbeats*. This was the start of my close relationship with the music that had mesmerized me over the preceding decade.

I was to leave The Downbeats about a year later. They were moving in a different direction and other players were being sought. But I did join the Musicians' Union.

While playing for the union, they had sent me with a quartet to Cranston, Rhode Island for a Bar Mitzvah at the Knights of Columbus Hall.

When we arrived, we found there was no Bar Mitzvah nor were there even any Jewish people.

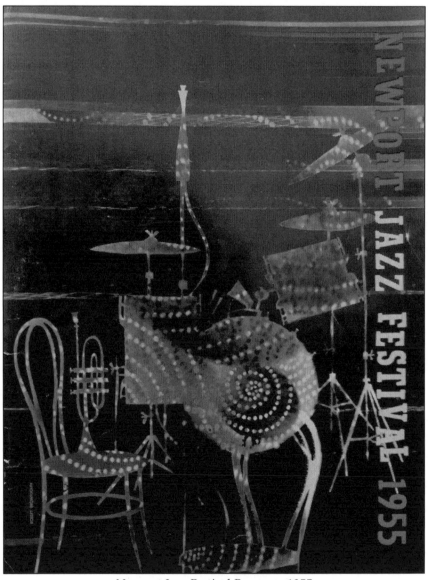

Newport Jazz Festival Program, 1955

I immediately telephoned the Ralph Stewart Union Office to complain. They said, "Play anyway… and don't forget to get the check."

Another time, they sent my group to a wedding in Valley Falls, Rhode Island. It turned out to be a Polish wedding. We were not prepared for polkas. All we knew was *She's Too Fat for Me*. We played that tune all night long, taking turns soloing and improvising the best we could.

In our own way, we imitated the great musicians, playing their numbers from the charts printed in fake books. We had fun performing and the experience lead me to a plethora of other musical opportunities.

Before too long, the second festival was announced. It had already outgrown the Newport Casino, and was to be moved to Freebody Park, almost next door, to accommodate a larger projected crowd.

Freebody Park was a city-owned athletic field surrounded by brick, stone and mortar, with bleachers and open space.

I purchased tickets right away.

The Lorillards wanted to include a Friday evening concert and they quickly sold out the show, which featured The Woody Herman Orchestra with his so-called "Third Herd" with Teddi King on vocals.

The Downbeats, 1958
(L-R) Gerry Schwartz, Sumner Fishbein, Burt Jagolinzer, and Fred Dupuis

Woody was at the top of his performance inserting the famous clarinet solos that we all had come to hear and see. We were not disappointed.

The dynamic Erroll Garner Trio was added. Erroll's interpretations and original compositions thrilled the audience. Only Erroll could deliver the piano improvisations that always made his gigs so unusual and attractive.

I had seen Erroll perform that past November at a social club, The Frolics, in Salisbury Beach, Massachusetts, with my cousin Merrill.

A funny incident happened after that concert. I hung around to get Erroll's autograph and hoped to maybe say a few words to him.

As it turned out, he was not in a very talkative mood, obviously tired from the performance. I commended him for a terrific presentation and asked him kindly for an autograph.

He quickly turned around, picked-up the big Yellow Pages telephone book that he had been sitting on during the performance, reached forward to grab my pen and scribbled the name *Erroll* across its front cover. He then handed it to me and said "Here Kid, here's your autograph."

I found out later that Erroll used a Chicago Yellow Pages telephone book to sit on at every gig. His book quickly became a prized item to me.

Unfortunately, over the years, I was to lose track of it. But the memory of that incident will always be with me.

Following Errol that night on the Newport stage was Stan Rubin and The Tigertown Five from Princeton University. Then came intermission.

The sound system at the park was not good and many people complained about it. I positioned myself close to a speaker to get the best sound that was available.

When the intermission was completed the great Coleman Hawkins on sax shared the stage with Roy Eldridge and his horn. Soon they were joined by the talented vocals of Joe Turner. What a session that was.

And if that wasn't enough, Louis Armstrong and his Orchestra followed featuring the voice of Velma Middleton. Louie captured the fans with his singing, scatting, and trumpet selections.

Accompanying Louis were his usual favorites, Billy Kyle on piano, Arvell Shaw at bass, Barney Bigard on clarinet, Trummy Young on Trombone and Barrett Deems on drums.

Topping the evening was an ending jam featuring a Jazz Festival All-Star Group led by Louis Armstrong on horn, with Coleman Hawkins on tenor, Roy Eldridge on trumpet, Woody Herman on the clarinet and Erroll Garner at the keyboard. What an ending. I'll never forget it.

After the show I was to run into Lucille and Louis on their way out of the park. I shook Louis' hands and Lucille hugged me.

♫ ♫ ♫

I thought that Saturday's show couldn't possibly beat Friday's blowout. I was in for a surprise.

Saturday's program opened with an unknown group led by drummer Max Roach featuring the trumpet of Clifford Brown.

Clifford Brown was a young gifted horn player who easily blended with the music of this performance. Little did anyone know that he was to die tragically a short time later at the age of just twenty-five.

Joining them were Harold Land on tenor, Rich Powell at the keyboard and George Morrow on bass.

The gifted sounds of Marian and Jimmy McPartland followed, with Marian at the piano and Jimmy on horn. Accompanying them was the veteran Joe Morrello on drums. I remember how rare it was for female jazz instrumentalist to be featured here at the festival.

Marian more than entertained us with her action at the keyboard, proving her excellent contribution to this emerging art form.

Then, Ruby Braff appeared with his cornet. Bob Brookmeyer followed on valve-trombone, along with Al Cohn on tenor. This proved to be one of the first major concerts for each of them. They absolutely blew us away.

Ruby's sound was very different. You could always recognize his work, and it was true quality.

Before intermission we were privy to the vocals of the great Dinah Washington accompanied by Max Roach on drums and Clifford Brown on horn.

Dinah, for the most part, sang songs that had not yet been recorded. Her personal flair was well received. I had now become a Dinah fan.

After the intermission, Chet Baker's special trumpet blended beautifully with the keyboard excellence of Russ Freeman. Jack Lawler performed on bass with Peter Littman on drums.

The saxophones of Lee Konitz and Wayne Marsh joined Baker's group. The sound became instantly louder and even more defined.

The stage emptied, and out walked the controversial and gifted Miles Davis. For some reason he was not listed in the festival program booklet. But he was about to steal the show.

Along with Miles came reedmen Zoot Sims and Gerry Mulligan. Others following were Percy Heath on bass, Connie Kay on drums and Thelonious Monk on the ivories.

It became a very memorable moment, which gave Miles the chance he needed to get back on top. He had been away for a while and many thought he was finished with music. On the contrary, he was to blow the place apart with the help of his spectacular accompanying team.

The new Miles had arrived. And I had been there to see it happen.

Next out to perform was a group made up of Wild Bill Davidson on horn, Pee Wee Russell on clarinet, Milt Hinton on the bass, festival director George Wein on piano and Vic Dickenson on the trombone. This was to be the beginning of the now famous Newport Jazz All-Stars.

This collection of performers gave improvisation a new meaning. Sheet music was nowhere to be found. Their combined talents proved to be upbeat and delightful.

But the best was yet to come. It was the end when all the performers came back on stage to jam.

Try to picture five raging trumpets, four saxes, a clarinetist and two trombones, accompanied by piano, bass and drums. They were truly some of the finest jazz musicians the world has ever known performing there, together, right in front of us. Wow!

Their sound was overpowering but exciting. I had never heard jazz at this level. It was truly jazz at its richest setting, a new standard had been set for gatherings in the future.

♫ ♫ ♫

The Saturday afternoon panel discussion was a workshop entitled "Jazz from the Outside-In" chaired by Father O'Connor.

Participants included two jazz historians, an editor, a composer, and a psychiatrist.

The forum took place at Belcourt Castle, a famous mansion down the street, just a few minutes away from the stage. It had been built by the great nineteenth century architect, Richard Morris Hunt for the wealthy railroad magnates, the Oliver Hazard Belmont family. The Lorillards had recently purchased it.

The panel talked about creating publicity to bring people to jazz. I concluded that jazz alone would bring people to the art form. But many attending saw value in the session. I couldn't find much to talk about.

♫ ♫ ♫

Sunday's event began with Duke Ellington at the microphone. He introduced the Modern Jazz Quartet. It was to be my first exposure to this group. I was taken by their totally new approach to jazz.

Featured were John Lewis on the ivories, Percy Heath on bass, with Milt Jackson on vibraphone and Connie Kay at the drums. I was challenged by their unusual sound.

Then, the Count Basie Band moved onto the stage. Bill Basie was to perform at the piano featuring the great Lester Young on tenor and Buck Clayton on horn, accompanied by Joe Jones on drums. Added to this group was a young Gerry Mulligan on deep reeds. Despite the house sound problems, the performance created an indelible, high-quality musical mix.

The Dave Brubeck Quartet followed. Accompanying Dave at the keyboard were Paul Desmond on the alto, Bob Bates on bass and Joe Dodge on the drums.

The sound of the Brubeck Quartet was quite new to me and to several of my close friends. At first, it was difficult to appreciate Dave's entire musical objectives. His classical interludes and touches were very modern and seemed to fit into some of the mainstream. But it was Paul Desmond's alto solos of *Take Five* that brought acceptance of the complete versatility of Brubeck's arrangements and sounds.

And it was Desmond's solo of *Take Five* that was to bring down the house at this early Newport festival. It remains, to many avid fans, one of the top highlights of all the historical jazz happenings to occur at Newport.

After this intermission, Billy Taylor was ready to perform at piano. He was to lead a group that included the sweet horn of Bobby Hackett, with the two bones of Kai Winding and J. J. Johnson. The reeds were played by Ben Webster on tenor, Bud Shank on the alto and Peanuts Hucko on clarinet. Johnny Smith supplemented on guitar.

This combination got the young crowd beating on their seats. I began beating on my seat as well.

The full Count Basie Orchestra was to finish off the evening featuring the incomparable voice of Joe Williams. It proved to be Basie and Joe at their very best.

No one could sing like Joe Williams. A woman in front of me began "swooning." How could anyone not like the voice of Joe Williams?

Another festival was over, and I remember leaving the park soaked and tired to the bounce of the Basie Band, and humming *Silk Stockings.*

Chapter 6
Rhode Island Jazz

In the early days, there were some great jazz radio stations. Veterans like Jim Mendes and Ron Della Chiesa gave us jazz music and educated us along the way. Their contributions for the listening crowd will always be fondly remembered.

And then there was Carl's Diggin's record shop on North Main Street in Providence where we purchased new and old playable records.

It was at about this time that I started attending local jazz events. I had joined the Newport Friends of Jazz, an organization run by Bill Angel, an aging enthusiast who had been spending a great deal of his time and energy bringing quality jazz to Newport. Bill had connections to many veteran performers, from New York City, Boston, and other locations around New England.

Rhode Island jazz singer to put on show on island

By James J. Gillis
Daily News staff

MIDDLETOWN — It's been a few years since singer Clay Osborne, 73, has had a jazz gig in the Newport area.

"I'd like to get down there more often, but Billy Weston gets all the gigs," Osborne said. "I'm just kidding. I like Billy. I do a lot of weddings in Newport, in those little mansions. What am I saying? Those big mansions, I should say."

The Providence-based Osborne gets to Aquidneck Island Sunday, for a show at the Royal Plaza Hotel at 425 East Main Road with pianist John Harrison. Sponsored by the Newport Jazz Society, the show runs from 2 to 6 p.m. Tickets are $8 for jazz society members and $10 for non-members.

Osborne has been singing professionally for more than 50 years, honing his craft in church as a boy and performing jazz tunes in nightclubs through the decades. "I do the old sentimental kind of jazz songs that you don't hear so often," he said. "I do the kind the older people like. I have quite a variety. My younger brother Jeffrey, he has a whole different sound."

Clay Osborne

Clay Osborne is the oldest of 12 kids. He is about 20 years older than youngest sibling Jeffrey Osborne, who amassed several Top 40 soul and R&B hits in the 1980s, including "On the Wings of Love" in 1982.

"He came up in a different generation than me," Clay Osborne said.

The older Osborne balanced his performing life with his career as a jewelry salesman. "I had chances (with music) through the years,"

he said. "But I never liked to go on the road that much. I liked staying close to home."

Two years ago, doctors amputated Osborne's lower legs because of circulatory problems. Now he sings from his wheelchair. "I went into a funk for about six months after losing my legs," he said. "But I have all these family members who pulled me out of it. I finally called a friend of mine and said, 'Do you need a singer?' And that's when I came back."

Sunday's show is the second for the fledgling Newport Jazz Society. Last month, a band featuring saxophonist Greg Abate, pianist Mac Chrupcala and singer Billy Weston drew more than 100 people to the Royal Plaza. The society is planning a Latin-flavored show for next month.

"We're very fortunate to have Clay Osborne this time," said Burt Jagolinzer, the group's president. "He is a great interpreter of the American songbook, in a way similar to Mel Tormé. He could've gone anywhere, but he is close to his family and wanted to stay in Rhode Island. It's the rest of the world's loss as far as I'm concerned."

Over the years, he was able to bring to Newport an impressive list of artists including the great pianist Ray Bryant, noted trumpeter Shorty Rogers, veteran tenor Bob Kindred, trumpeter Herb Pomeroy (who had played with Charlie Parker), pianist great Junior Mance, the multi-talented Clark Terry, New York City's most popular clarinetist Ken Peplowski, and the extraordinary pianist Monty Alexander. These events primarily took place at the Hotel Viking.

He was also responsible for performances from Greater Rhode Island talent that included the tenor of Scott Hamilton, the voice of Shawnn Monteiro, the reeds of Harry Allen, the voice of Steve Marvin, the multi-talented Diamond Centofanti, the voice of Patty Loncar, the reeds of Dick Johnson, the voice of Clay Osborne, the reeds of Art Manchester and Greg Abate, the voice of Bonnie Mann, the ultra-sweet trumpets of Lou Colombo and Jeff Stout, and the voices of Ronnie Rose and Rebecca Parris, the talented bass of Paul Del Nero, the trombone of Kenny Wenzel, and the voice of Carol Sloane... just to name a few.

Bill Angel would induce the "out-of-towners" to come to Newport for a free weekend, at one of the many wonderful local hotels and he paid them small amounts for their performances. This proved to be a smart way to get these big-city talents to come without having to give them their usual large paychecks.

Bill was forced to operate on a shoe-string. Yet, the music somehow continued, often funded with his own money.

We enjoyed wonderful opportunities to meet and converse with the performers during breaks. Many pictures and autographs were exchanged. Each one of these musicians helped educate the audience and their talents represented jazz at an excellent level.

We felt very special. How lucky we were.

"Three Guys from Providence"
Burt Jagolinzer, Scott Hamilton & Kenny Jagolinzer

Local pianist Mac Chrupcala operated another attractive program in more recent years, but on a different basis.

No membership was required. We had to just come to the Atlantic Beach Club in Middletown or the Treadway Inn in Newport and buy a drink or two, and maybe some food, to help pay for the band and keep the club owner happy.

Mac, an excellent veteran pianist and former trombone player, had developed an organization that had captured a large portion of the musical needs for social engagements in the greater Newport area. He is probably best known as the creator of the Sunday afternoon jazz performance that regularly featured his own quartet, with Alan Bernstein on bass, Artie Cabral on drums and the late Billy Weston on vocals and trumpet, and usually accompanied by a guest talent. It became a winner.

Among his many invites included harmonica jazz great Mike Turk, the veteran trombonist George Masso, reed masters Greg Abate, Freddie DeCristofaro, Artie Krakowski, Carl Hosband, Joe Esposito and Kirk Feather; trumpeters Curt Ramm, Eric Bloom, Jeff Stout and John Allmark; singers Marlene Verplanck, Annette Sanders, Bonnie Mann, Amanda Carr, Marcelle Gauvin and Daryl Sherman (often with the spectacular Mike Renzi at the ivories); local talented songstress and entertainer Nancy Paolino (Mac's wife); George Zecher on the steel cans, popular drummers Mike Coffey, Vinnie Pagano and the late Jack Menna, bassists Tom Pasquarelli and Dave Zinno, and the noted Canadian vibes player Warren Chiasson.

(Among the regular patrons, who like me, enjoyed the music at the Atlantic Beach Club were my pals, Giggsy, M. J. Harris and Horty, Phyllis and Joe, Judy, Deb Lucente, Lou, Teresa and

Andy, Carol Gates and Pat King, Norma, Esther Bernstein, El-
len, John, Linda, Frank and Debbie and Peter K., the owner.
And, you can't leave out loyal bartenders Randy, Billy and
Heather!)

Mac's Sunday gigs continue today at The Atlantic Beach Club,
September through May.

Unfortunately, Bill Angel passed away in the late 1990's. A few
years later I was encouraged to take over Bill Angel's dormant
concept. I called for a meeting of those that might be interested.

We decided to change the name to *The Newport Jazz Association*. I
was elected the non-profit organization's president. For the next
couple of years we produced some quality local jazz happenings.

It was fun and it helped supplement the other local music available in Greater Newport.

We donated some needed funds to the local schools so they
could purchase sheet music and supplies, and we supported the
local music union and donated to their annual scholarship fund.

And, of course, we promoted the jazz festival itself. We even offered our services to them many years ago. Our basic goal has
always been to "help keep jazz alive in the area." We have always done our best to do just that.

Unfortunately in recent years, the climate of financial support has dwindled and the economy has taken its toll on the association's current activities. But, we still exist, waiting for our chance to surface, once again to help the jazz art form at the local level.

Our organization has also been honoring important individuals who have contributed to the promotion of jazz in the Newport area. Each has been elected and enshrined into our Newport Jazz Association's Hall-of-Fame. Inductees include the late Elaine Lorillard, George Wein, Saucy Silvia (former head of the local union and a dynamic cabaret singer), pianist Bill Angel (in memoriam), and Mac Chrupcala.

Additional jazz happenings in Newport could be found at The Hotel Viking, The DoubleTree, The Treadway Inn, and some regular gigs at The Inn at Castle Hill, OceanCliff and The Cliff Walk Manor (now known as The Chanler.)

You could often find the late Matthew Quinn at the piano, often with Richie Haddocks on bass and Stormin' Norman Jackson on the sticks, at several places around the community. Stormin' Norman had spent several years with the Illinois Jacquet Orchestra performing around the world.

Then there was Gene Oliver at the ivories down at The Astor Restaurant's pub. And dynamic saxophonist Willy Love could be often found at the Red Parrot, at the base of Memorial Boulevard where it meets Lower Thames Street.

And there was also Art Manchester with his reeds and John Monllos on guitar at The Canfield House near Bellevue Avenue.

And we can't forget Al Wilson at the Atlantic Beach Club every Saturday evening with Stan Ellis on the sticks and Dennis Pratt on bass.

Today, in the Newport vicinity, you can locate jazz flowing from the work of pianist and promoter Mac Chrupcala, promoter Dick Lupino, bass player and singer, Lois Vaughan, and promoter and drummer Bob Saraceno. These musicians often feature outsiders to supplement their own talent.

Back a few years ago, you might also have found pianist and cabaret singer Pat Mitchell, often at The Hotel Viking, and sometimes R. J. Von See on bass, or Art Manchester on reeds, with Milt Javery on the ivories and even Bob Helmbrecht on bass with Billy Weston on trumpet. In those days the mixing of talent was often the case, more so than today.

The former mayor of Newport, The Honorable Richard Sardella, owns Sardella's Restaurant, an excellent restaurant on Memorial Boulevard. He specializes in Northern Italian cuisine, homemade on the premises. Richard has always had love for jazz. He graciously allowed Matthew Quinn to begin regular jazz programs on Wednesday evenings in the main dining room. After

Matthew's unfortunate passing, Dick Lupino carried on the tradition, bringing regular local talent and others to this Wednesday happening.

Dennis Cook, the multi-talented reed player and Yvonne Monette's voice and piano can be found quite regularly even today at Sardella's.

Nancy (Parker) Wilson, manager of The Greenvale Vineyard in Portsmouth, has always had love for jazz and opened up her facility for a Saturday afternoon jazz program. Once again Matthew Quinn began bringing quality local talent to perform while customers were tasting Greenvale's excellent wines. It became a real happening, Dick Lupino also continued this gig, choosing an array of veteran talent to perform each Saturday. (Among the regular applauding patrons are Kia, Janet, Rena, Jennifer Wells, Trish Nordeen, Ed Gardella and his wife, Joe Romano and Joan, Esther, Linda, Debbie, Nancy and Fred.) Today, it is still a terrific experience just a few minutes from downtown Newport.

Dick Lupino currently holds musical court on Friday evenings at The Chanler, hiring excellent musicians to supplement his singing and bass playing. Jazz patrons regularly include Frank, Nikki, Peter, Ken and Marty, Trish, and Rick and Jennifer, and the wonderful bartenders, Maurice and Teddy and others.

It is tight seating but Nancy and I always find a spot to do some dancing.

I would visit great spots for jazz in the Providence area as well. They included Bobby's Rollaway in Pawtucket, The Gatehouse, Asquino's Restaurant in East Providence, Alary's, The Manhattan, Capriccio's, Olive's, Bumble Bee's and others.

Asquino's Restaurant was where I first came upon the late Clay Osborne, as part of the JK Trio. He was a talented pianist with a terrific emotional voice.

Many of us believed that Clay could have easily become one of the world's greatest male jazz singers, but being the oldest of a large Providence family, he was needed to stay local and help raise his family. Though Clay did sneak away to sing with John Allmark's Band in Saratoga, New York at the 1998 JVC-New York Jazz Festival.

As it turned out, two of his younger brothers did become internationally famous. Billy Osborne became an excellent pianist, composer and arranger, spending many years in Hollywood and touring with the Ray Charles Orchestra all around the world. His youngest brother Jeffrey Osborne, is today, a prominent pop singer and recording artist.

Fortunately, Clay's talent was appreciated locally and he established a loyal following.

As part of that group, we regularly visited his performances. It became a highlight of my weekly jazz infusion.

Late in his career both of his legs had to be amputated because of poor circulation, but it never stopped him from performing. He would arrive in his specially-equipped vehicle and use a wheelchair to maintain his independence.

Clay gave up piano playing to focus seriously on singing. He became the complete master of the American Song Book. As followers, we cherished his emotional renditions of many of jazz's most important tunes. Often tears were seen in the eyes of our group because of his performances.

He appeared at several locations around greater Providence including The Wharf Tavern in Warren, The Cheeky Monkey in Newport, The Gatehouse Restaurant in Providence, Bovi's Restaurant in East Providence and many others.

Clay was often accompanied by the talents of John Harrison or Yvonne Monette at the piano and Tom Pasquarelli on bass.

His gig at The Gatehouse Restaurant, where they named the lounge area "The Clay Osborne Room," lasted many years.

For those years it became the best ticket in town. How lucky we had been to easily enjoy one of the finest jazz talents possibly in the country, with a minimum of expense, regularly in our hometown.

Clay passed away on April 11, 2006 after an extended illness. We treasured those special nights and the memories that came with them.

At the Gatehouse, I met other jazz lovers including Dinah Baker, Annette Clayborn, Dr. Mary Palmer, Carol Rovinski, Bob Parenti, Nancy Parenti, Harry Glaser, Craig Miller, Robin Boucher, Carol Thornton, Red Lenox, and Mary Bogan and her mother. Most of them are longtime friends and excellent listeners. Dinah knows just about everybody and is a key enthusiast. Annette never missed a jazz beat, reciting every lyric ever written. She passed away last spring, after a long illness.

Red Lenox and the late Bob Parenti played mean horns and were always there with Bob's wife Nancy to support good jazz.

Clay's student singers, Cassandra McKinley and Mary Bogan, got their starts here, too.

For decades, Bovi's Restaurant in East Providence has been the place to find big band music at its best. John Allmark with his spectacular trumpet, leads and directs this special group of quality musicians. On Monday evenings starting at 9 p.m. they light-up this limited-seating pub with wonderful arrangements of the American standards and more. Currently it is the best jazz ticket available. Come early as seating is often standing-room-only.

At the top of our tiny state is the City of Woonsocket, and home to the formidable Chan's Chinese Restaurant. Here, owner John Chan has welcomed top jazz performances over the past several decades. His love for the performers, plus his love for jazz in general, has made his establishment one of the longest running places continually available for our art form. Most of our local musicians have played there and a few continue to do so even today. You can often find the voice of Marcelle Gauvin, the reeds of Greg Abate and Dan Moretti, the strings of John Wheatley, the voices and cabaret of Debra Mann and Daryl Sherman, and the wonderful voices of Carol Sloane or Rebecca Parris with Peter Kontrimas on bass performing here.

There was once an excellent lounge in Providence called the High Hat where management scheduled Tuesdays for jazz. Jazz veteran Vinny Pagano hired the talent to complement himself at the drums. He was able to bring great talent, each week, to perform, including the voices of Amanda Carr and Tish Adams, the cabaret and pianists Paul Broadnax, Tim Ray and Mike Renzi, the voices of Barbara Slater, Bob Manelli and Rachel Price, bassists Peter Kontrimas, Marty Ballou and Dave Zinno and many more quality entertainers from the Boston and New York areas.

It was a terrific place to watch and enjoy jazz, at its best. The sound system and stage arrangements were excellent, with good lighting and darn good food. The cost was very reasonable and there was plenty of room for dancing. The people who ran it were friendly, hospitable and caring. Those of us who came there always got their money's worth.

Unfortunately, when one of the owners passed away, the new ownership decided to change the restaurant's format to pop and rhythm and blues. It was a major loss to the Rhode Island jazz scene.

The SideBar Lounge then began to hire jazz, but it was not the same. And it didn't last very long, either. For about a year, management tried jazz and it did prove to be a springboard for some. Many local musicians performed there.

But for whatever real reason, probably money, they decided to move towards Latin and rock. Slowly, traditional jazz faded away from this club scene and once again the true, local jazz fans got the boot.

But on that springboard came the ambitious Barbara Slater. Barbara is already an accomplished attorney, and noted author with a television and media background, who had decided to become a jazz singer. She studied hard and researched the art form. Determined to develop her inner skills, she took voice lessons from several veterans and has paid her dues, so to speak. Much of her growth took place at the SideBar Lounge.

Working with excellent coaches like jazz pianist and arranger Kent Hewitt, and several others, she has been able to turn the corner into a professional career, if she wants one.

Barbara has developed into a terrific jazz singer accentuating the American Song Book. She has conquered the challenge of singing with the big band and in the smaller groups as well. Her deep and unusual voice reminds me of the late June Christy.

Others have had their skills honed at the SideBar, too, including young Eric Bloom, whose trumpet solos sound like those of Providence's late great Bobby Hackett or maybe even Doc Severinsen of Johnny Carson's Tonight Show fame.

Eric has already been touted around the country and his professional future has been on the rise for the last several years. I think we'll all be hearing much more from Eric Bloom.

And I can't leave out the work of drummer, John Bedessa, and his group that helped keep jazz alive at The Sidebar. Even former Providence Mayor, Buddy Cianci, played the drums with him on occasion.

As you can see, Rhode Island has produced a large number of talented musicians, and jazz continues to flow through this tiny state in unpredictable places with unpredictable performers. There is a need for a place and an organization to stabilize jazz's existence in Rhode Island, and to perpetuate its future.

And certainly Newport, just because of its annual festivals for some sixty years, must be considered second in the pecking order of importance behind only New Orleans. Behind Newport I would rank Kansas City, Memphis, St. Louis, Chicago, New York, and Boston, probably in that order.

Chapter 7
Perpetuating the History of Jazz

A few years before the Newport Jazz Festival's founder Elaine Lorillard's passing, she spoke to me about creating a jazz museum in Newport, Rhode Island.

She wanted a place to display her historic collection of memorabilia from the Newport Jazz Festivals. And Elaine wanted to create a special place for local musicians to perform daily, and to supplement those performances with quality musicians from around the world, to perform throughout the calendar year.

She had hoped to get financial support for the project from the State of Rhode Island and the City of Newport. Her son, Pierre Lorillard, offered to donate funds to help get the campaign going.

Elaine had asked me, as president of the Newport Jazz Association, and my vice president, R. J. von See, to serve on the first board of directors. We had even discussed possible locations in the Newport area.

Unfortunately, Elaine died before the project could be started.

George Wein's Hall of Fame Certificate

I recently visited Kansas City, and in particular, their important jazz museum, at 18th and Vine Street, which focuses mostly on the pre-1950's era. Jazz history from this time forward belongs in Newport, Rhode Island, where the Lorillards and George

Wein began a new approach, fostering a growth in the art form thought previously unattainable.

It was Newport and George Wein that brought jazz to its peak of popularity and world acclaim.

Newport jazz needs a permanent location, a building where jazz can always be found. Visitors to Rhode Island, and especially Newport, have difficulty trying to find jazz, in any form as most of the locations described earlier have closed.

Newport is known for sailing, beaches, mansions, tennis and jazz. Jazz is the only feature without a central location. This should not be. Newport deserves to have a permanent home for jazz if for no other reason than Elaine Lorillard wanted one.

Kansas City's museum was spearheaded with support from the state and city. And they were fortunate to have a special list of prominent individuals who donated substantial funding.

And now St. Louis, which was the cradle for blues, is in the process of creating a home for a permanent blues museum.

It is time Newport, Rhode Island had such a museum, too.

Maybe this message will get to the State of Rhode Island and the City of Newport, so they can work toward this objective. I would personally support such a drive -- with vigor.

If such a fund is started, a portion of the sale of this book will be donated to the effort towards this accomplishment.

Let us not forget that most of the great jazz musicians to ever play their instruments performed here in Newport. Their personal advancements came from their work on the Newport stage. Many owe their success to having performed here. This is a special and important historical location, very worthy of a permanent home.

Chapter 8
Friday Evenings at the Casino

While the bulk of the jazz festival performances were always scheduled on Saturday and Sunday afternoons, the Friday night programs were often the highlight of the weekend events.

The Newport Casino which housed the first Newport Jazz Festival in 1954 was the perfect setting for these special Friday evening happenings.

Producers smartly kept the Friday programs on a singular status. Though it was in a way a happening unto itself, promoters used it to draw fans to the rest of the weekend and the total jazz schedule.

Friday evenings somehow became a rather dressy event, and many people wore their finest. Some still come to the festival events in gowns, suits, ties and their Sunday best. But the Saturday's and Sunday's dress is usually dictated by the weather. Most attended in sport clothes, often in shorts, prepared for the comfort of the open field.

Count Basie

Through the years many of jazz's greatest talents performed in this special setting.

Among the Friday evening performers over the years were Louis Armstrong (with Gerry Mulligan and Dizzy Gillespie), crooner Mel Torme, The Dave Brubeck Quartet, The Manhattan Transfer, singer Harry Connick, Jr. and his orchestra, trumpeter Wynton Marsalis, Diana Krall, Tony Bennett with K.D. Lang, Blossom Dearie, The Count Basie Orchestra, cabaret singer Bobby Short, and trumpeter Chris Botti and his orchestra, to name a few.

Each graced the audience of this limited-seating gathering with their own very special performances. How lucky we are to have been entertained in such a beautiful setting over the years.

On many Fridays, we had to deal with rain, fog, high-humidity and strong winds. But these events still took place, and the great jazz fans stayed in their seats despite the weather.

To help create a worthy social atmosphere, management offered a limited cocktail party prior to the Friday evening event. Sponsors and vendors offered samples of wine and delicious food with terrific local jazz performers gaining exposure. This party gave attendees an early chance to dance and imbibe, preparing them for the main events that were to follow.

Chapter 9
The 1956 Newport Jazz Festival

The 1956 Newport Jazz Festival began on a Thursday evening. And the heavens opened up.

It poured, and once again we got soaked, very soaked. This time I remembered to bring along a hat and umbrella yet somehow still found a way to get soaked.

I remember the famous bass player Charlie Mingus, with a group continuing through the storm, playing upbeat tunes that kept everyone reasonably happy. The Mingus compositions were new to me. I had several of his records, but none contained these melodies.

The weekend highlight was the Saturday performance of The Duke Ellington Orchestra.

Usually a Master of Ceremonies would introduce the performance, sometimes giving the audience a bit of background. Duke himself was picked to be MC that night and he took the time to give excellent background on each key soloist, plus interesting facts about each piece itself.

To that point in my young career, I hadn't seen a leader do that.

I was very impressed with Duke and his method. Others were to follow his approach but only Duke could do it with class and with the proper information.

The orchestra played Duke's and Billy Strayhorn's well-known numbers, *Sophisticated Lady* and *Mood Indigo*.

(Strayhorn was known as a pianist, composer, arranger and sidekick to Duke. Later, I was to spend time with him and Duke in a very unusual setting.)

Then the Orchestra presented *Diminuendo in Blue* and *Crescendo in Blue*. These numbers captured the weekend.

Little did we know that this performance was to become not only a signature of The Duke Ellington Orchestra but it helped single out the Newport Jazz Festival as THE place for musicians to perform from around the world.

Even former President Bill Clinton, at a local Rhode Island event, mentioned his desire as a young saxophone player back in Arkansas to someday perform on stage at Newport.

Anita O'Day

But it was Duke's tenor soloist, Paul Gonsalves who stole the show. He performed some seven choruses without stopping. And Duke just let him go… and go he did.

A blonde woman jumped up and began swinging in the aisle. Others quickly joined her. Soon, the whole crowd was jitterbugging and swinging. And I was one of them.

Paul Gonsalves kept playing. The fans loved it. The audience kept clapping. It became a great memory of an emerging art form.

I felt very lucky to have been there, and to have taken part in the swinging. Not only does it remain among my fondest festival memories, but it was to become one of the greatest highlights in Newport Festival history.

There were many other performers during that weekend, too, including the Chico Hamilton Band, songstress Anita O'Day, the Joe Jones Trio and the Bud Shank Quartet.

But nothing was to compare to the Duke Ellington Orchestra and the spectacular solos that Duke delivered that night. Duke was to end the evening by telling the audience, "I love you madly." It was to become a saying that many musicians still use today.

On the way home from this festival, I realized that I had been once again witness to some of jazz's special moments and lasting history.

Chapter 10
My Friendship with Joyce Wein

It was during one of the earliest festivals that I had the occasion to first meet Joyce Wein, George's important other half.

Joyce was meandering around the stage area when she stopped me. I was wearing a large jazz pin that had caught her eye. The pin was a giveaway to fans who had attended one of the previous festivals. It advertised Schlitz Beer, which at the time, had been a major sponsor for her husband George.

She was collecting memorabilia from various performances, and it was obvious that she had designs on my pin.

And so, I simply gave it to her. She offered to pay me for it, but of course, I refused to accept any money. It was to be the beginning of a long friendship.

Through the years, I was able to procure additional pins and items for her. It became an annual rite for me to meet with Joyce at Newport, and to pass on interesting items to help supplement her expanding collection.

We became special friends. Welcoming hugs and kisses were part of our greetings. And then we would talk jazz and exchange local chatter about each year's weather, talent and the unique problems that seem to always come with Newport's programs.

Joyce's death in 2005, at the age of 76, was painful for me. Our meetings had become a regular and important part of each festival. I won't forget her unique soft voice, wonderful smile and meaningful hugs.

In George's book, *Myself Among Others*, he tells us about his relationship with Joyce and her importance to his success.

Those of us who had the good fortune to have known her will not easily forget her.

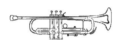

Chapter 11
The 1957 Newport Jazz Festival

The 1957 Newport Festival featured Louis Armstrong. They planned to celebrate his fifty-seventh birthday. A birthday cake was actually brought out onto the stage. There was no sign of balloons.

I can remember the pre-program which featured the Farmington, Connecticut High School Band with Marshall Brown conducting. These young students were terrific. Their arrangements and solos were very professional. It set the stage for a great concert to come.

Songwriter Johnny Mercer was introduced, and Ella Fitzgerald began singing many of his compositions, accompanied by Henry "Red" Allen on trumpet and Jack Teagarden on trombone. It was wonderful, and the set highlighted my day.

Billie Holiday performed, too, and so did Carmen McRae.

Today I recognize how special this day was, having Billie, Carmen and Ella on one afternoon singing both separately and together. Imagine, three of the finest female jazz singers in the history of the art form together on the same stage at Newport. How lucky we were.

But it was Louis who came out to sing a duet with Ella that brought down the house. Their fans were delighted, and so was I.

Louis was nearing the end of his long career and now mostly used just his voice to perform. His trumpet playing was limited, and it was evident during his performance.

But Louis being Louis, he still captured the large audience and no one felt cheated.

Others performing that year included the be-bop team called The Jazz Laboratory featuring Gigi Gryce on saxophone and flute, with Donald Byrd on his mean trumpet.

During one of the intermissions, I had the opportunity to shake hands with composer Johnny Mercer, as did hundreds of others who had waited in line for the chance.

I also had the opportunity to meet with Lucille Armstrong. We had met now at all three festivals. Once again, she gave me a hug. She made me feel very special and connected.

Chapter 12
The 1958 Newport Jazz Festival
At Freebody Park

The 1958 festival expanded to four days, and Thursday's performance began with a tribute to "Duke" Edward Kennedy Ellington. Duke's contributions to jazz were already world renowned and everyone in the jazz world recognized his talents in both composition and performance, and his love for both the craft and the people connected to it. I was truly in awe of Ellington and his orchestra.

Close to the peak of his career, Duke had become a giant in the industry for his music, style and perfect grace. And his stage presentation was one-of-a-kind.

Louis Armstrong and Willis Conover

Gospel's finest, Mahalia Jackson, performed first. She brought tears to the eyes of many of us with her sacred cries of beauty and God, that brought everyone to focus. This religious adventure proved Gospel's place within the mainstream. It was truly a great, special moment.

Others on the card that night were trumpeter Miles Davis in a quintet, the great Marian McPartland Trio with Gerry Mulligan on baritone-sax, trumpeter Rex Stuart and the Dave Brubeck Quartet.

It was a superb evening, and I couldn't wait for Friday.

Burt Jagolinzer

♫ ♫ ♫

Friday evening featured Benny Goodman and his Orchestra, highlighting Zoot Sims and Seldon Powell on saxes, Bill Hodges and Taft Jordan on trumpets, Kenny Burrell on guitar, Arvell Shaw at the bass and Roland Hanna at the keyboard.

Jimmy Rushing (Mr. Side-By-Side) sang with the Goodman band. It was a terrific performance I'll never forget.

An all-star group gathered together for the ending. This included Miles, Mulligan, Zoot and Rex Stuart. It was sensational to say the least. It had been a great way to end Friday's program.

♫ ♫ ♫

Saturday night featured a huge variety of terrific artists. Leading the way was the voice of Joe Turner accompanied by Buddy Tate and Georgie Auld on tenor saxophones, Earl Warren was on alto, Buck Clayton on trumpet, Joe Jones on drums, Tony Scott on clarinet, Jack Teagarden on trombone and Gerry Mulligan on baritone sax.

It was an excellent mix and the sound was awesome.

The Ray Charles Sextet followed with Ray swinging at the ivories. It was a gasser.

Then Gerry Mulligan led his own quartet featuring Art Farmer on trumpet. We loved their work.

Following Gerry, Chuck Berry graced the stage with a group called The Newport Blues Band. He sang numbers that he had already made famous, and the fans applauded the revival.

After intermission, the Maynard Ferguson Orchestra blew us away. The group featured Slide Hampton on bone and Billy Chase on trumpet. Maynard's screeching horn hit high heaven to the delight of us all.

The voice of Dakota Staton followed with Jack Teagarden on trombone and the clarinet of Pee Wee Russell in duet.

It too, was a special evening, with plenty of terrific sounds professionally performed in front of a sellout crowd at Freebody Park.

Sunday offered two performances. The afternoon concert featured the Sonny Rollins Trio, Thelonious Monk on piano, Jack Teagarden on trombone and Pee Wee Russell on clarinet. And as expected, they were awesome.

Next up to perform was the Horace Silver Quintet, the Tony Scott Quintet, and pianist Billy Taylor in trio with Sonny Stitt and Lee Konitz on reeds and J. J. Johnson on trombone. It was truly a treat to witness and hear these multiple combinations.

♫ ♫ ♫

Sunday evening boasted the presentations of singers Chris Connor and Dinah Washington. These gals and their accompanists were outstanding. Their selections of tunes and deliveries were excellent.

Terri Gibbs, playing his vibes, with the voice of Billy Eckstine, drew second draw. The Max Roach Quartet followed. The George Shearing Quintet then made its mark.

Each of these groups performed wonderfully.

After intermission came Louis Armstrong and the All-Stars with Billy Kyle on piano and Barney Bigard on clarinet.

As usual, Louis stole the show. His grunts, squeaky voice and irregular-sounding trumpet got the place humming, stomping and clapping throughout the performance.

Louis proved to be a great choice for the ending of Sunday's concert and the festival's four-day program.

Another stellar happening had taken place in Newport.

Chapter 13
Jazz, A Major Influence on Integration

Since jazz's earliest rise in America, it has been a major important influence in African-American advancement toward racial equality.

I met Dr. Martin Luther King, Jr. at a Boston University lecture in the 1950's. I stayed after his moving speech to formally meet him.

He asked, "Why would a white boy like you come to listen to me tonight?"

My answer was deeply received. "I am sad over the divisions of people, and know that you have a great following... and also I am in love with your people's musical influence in jazz."

He quickly replied "Yes, jazz will help bring you together with my people." And not surprisingly, it has done so.

I truly recognize the contributions of individuals like George Wein, who married a Black girl. George, who cherished his late wife, Joyce, would not let segregation detour his determination to succeed in promoting his love for jazz. Joyce became the savior of his many dealings with prejudice and unjustness, particularly in the early years.

Few have given their lives to that cause like George Wein.

His book *Myself among Others* documents his musical life and the many racial and anti-Semitic issues he was forced to endure.

Chapter 14
The 1959 Newport Jazz Festival

The 1959 Newport Jazz Festival highlighted the performances of pianist Erroll Garner's Trio and The Duke Ellington Orchestra.

I attended the afternoon discussion group led by the lectures of Professor Sterling Brown entitled "The Roots of Jazz" and "Negroes in Jazz."

Brown was a noted professor of African-American Studies at Howard University for many years, and later at Vassar College, New York University, Atlanta University and Yale.

Although I didn't totally agree with the professor, it was very enlightening to hear his profound opinions.

The evening performance featured The Duke's Orchestra with the incomparable voice and gyrations of Jimmy Rushing, more commonly known as "Mr. Five-By-Five." Their gig was wonderful. We were beating and clapping throughout.

Also performing was the Marshall Brown Youth Band along with several other groups.

Marshall Brown had graduated from New York University and Columbia, attaining a Master's Degree in Music. He had spent most of his adult life working with high school and college youngsters developing quality performers who continue to excel in several of Marshall's performing orchestras.

This Youth Band displayed and performed at a very high level. Their sounds were extremely professional and the music selection was terrific.

Duke Ellington's orchestra came back on stage and finished-off the concert with several upbeat thrillers.

The crowd began leaving with the rhythm still ringing in their ears. We certainly got our money's worth from this concert. As usual, it was an outstanding event.

Chapter 15
U. S. Army & Music

I left my first year in pre-medical school at Providence College deciding it was time to serve my country. I enlisted in the United States Army.

While at Fort Dix, New Jersey I volunteered for the post marching band and the performing jazz band. It was to become a lot of fun, and it kept me away from the drudgery of everyday duty.

In that jazz group was a terrific sax player by the name of Cordine James who claimed to be the step-brother to trumpet great Harry James. I have lost track of him over the last thirty years, though I learned he had been traveling with the Buddy Rich Orchestra for several of those years.

I processed through basic-training at Fort Dix with the famous crooner Steve Lawrence, cartoonist, playwright and Broadway producer Herb Gardiner, and Stephen Rockefeller, who a short time later was to have disappeared somewhere in Africa.

Steve Lawrence had just begun dating singer Eydie Gorme. She would fly into Fort Dix in a helicopter most weekends. They would put on amazing shows in the Service Club that money couldn't buy.

Often they would attract other professional musicians to join them. Her gig at NBC on Steve Allen's "Tonight Show" in New York City attracted many terrific jazz musicians to perform with them at Fort Dix.

The list included Gerry Mulligan on reeds, J. J. Johnson on trombone and Miles Davis on horn.

A friend from Newport had reminded me of the approaching Newport Jazz Festival. Tickets were quickly procured for my group of close friends.

Having received a forty-eight hour pass from duty, I was driven by a fellow soldier to the Fort Lee, New Jersey edge of the George Washington Bridge.

There, I began hitch-hiking, looking for a ride, wearing my class-A uniform holding a cardboard sign that read: "NEW-PORT, R.I." I attracted a lot of attention.

Finally, a new-looking station wagon pulled over just in front of me. A smiling young Black man jumped out and asked, "Are you looking for a ride to the Newport Jazz Festival?" "Yes," I quickly replied. "Then come on in," he answered.

I entered the back seat and he jumped in beside me. I was so shocked to discover that this vehicle contained the great Duke Ellington in the right front seat with his son, Mercer Ellington, seated on my right. The seat to my left belonged to the famous composer and arranger, Billy Strayhorn. The driver was their featured saxophone soloist Paul Gonzales.

I thought I had died and had gone to heaven. Duke Ellington and his important band members had picked me up hitch-hiking. *Wow!*

Chapter 16
Hitchhiking with Duke

While traveling with Duke's group toward Newport, I sat quietly in the back seat with Mercer on one side and Billy Strayhorn on the other.

Strayhorn held a brown paper bag and he brought out a small ham sandwich. He offered me half. I graciously declined.

Minutes later he suggested enjoying a banana. I told him that, "I love bananas." He reached into the bag and presented me with a healthy looking bright yellow one.

Strayhorn took interest in my remarks about my "loving bananas." He asked me, "Why?" I told him that besides enjoying the taste, I recognized the beauty, its bold color and interesting form… and that nature had given this fruit a distinctive identification.

Many years later I was attending a special musical event at the Boston Museum of Fine Arts. It was a tribute to the music of the late Billy Strayhorn. The event included several local musicians and was promoted by Boston jazz radio personality Eric Jackson of WGBH Radio.

A side attraction at the event was David Hajdu the author of a new book about the life of Strayhorn entitled, *Lush Life*.

At intermission, I was fortunate to have an audience with David and I told him of my experience with Strayhorn. He was taken by my story. He said that if he had known earlier of my experience, my story would have been included in his book.

I purchased the book at the end of the event. Little did I know that Strayhorn had spent much of his time appreciating nature and nature's beauty. Several incidents in the book supported the unusual remarks Strayhorn made to me.

A few years after the Duke had passed away, I had the good fortune of attending a performance by the Ellington Orchestra in Boston. After their usual magnificent gig, I waited for a meeting with Mercer who had now been fronting his dad's famous band all over the world.

Duke Ellington had passed away in May 1974, at the age of 75. Some twelve thousand people attended his funeral. He is buried in the Bronx, New York.

Mercer came to my requested meeting wearing a broad Ellington smile on his face.

After commending his performance, I asked him if he remembered me as that young soldier whom he and his dad had picked up hitchhiking back in the 1960's.

He said he did, but I always wondered if he really remembered... or if he was just trying to be nice to me.

CHAPTER 17
The 1960 Newport Jazz Festival

The 1960 festival lasted for five days. It was to be a musical dream.

It started Thursday evening with Dave Brubeck's quartet. Charlie Mingus' quartet followed. Then came the Cannonball Adderley Quintet featuring his brother Nate Adderley at trumpet and Cannonball on the ivories. They blew the place apart. Wow!

Included in the evening was the romantic voice of Nina Simone, saxophonist Ornette Coleman (with his strange modern quartet,) the Art Farmer and Benny Golson group and an orchestra fronted by the great high-range trumpet player Maynard Ferguson.

Ferguson performed beyond his normal trumpet solos, hitting levels seemingly unachievable with a horn. It was different, and it drew the attention of many.

Many of us thought that Maynard was sure to have a bright future. I had the good fortune to have met him prior to his performance. We shook hands and we had our pictures taken by several onlookers.

Friday's performance featured Willie "The Lion" Smith, the Stride Piano, with several pianists including the legendary ragtime giant Eubie Blake at the keyboard.

Eubie, now in his seventies, had been noted as a composer, lyricist, and ragtime performer in his earliest days, at the turn of the twentieth century. The audience loved his unusual beat and skills.

♫ ♫ ♫

Saturday started with an afternoon performance by the Newport Youth Band directed by Marshall Brown. Following that great session came a group led by clarinetist Pee Wee Russell and the sweet trumpet sounds of Ruby Braff. It was awesome.

Then the Herbie Mann Sextet was to finish off a great afternoon.

The Saturday evening stage was filled with top-rated talent lead by The Oscar Peterson Quartet featuring Herb Ellis on guitar, and the mesmerizing voice of Dakota Staton with Harry "Sweets" Edison on horn.

Dave Brubeck and Paul Desmond

Then came the appearance of The Ray Charles Orchestra featuring The Rayettes, dancing, singing and accompanying Ray at the piano. Ray brought the house down with his incomparable showmanship. The place went wild. It was the closest to a Busby Berkeley theatrical film extravaganza ever performed at Newport.

The pianist and composer Horace Silver's Quintet made its mark next. Their sounds and talent were evident from the very first tune.

Also, on that evening's stage was a group featuring Ben Webster at his tenor saxophone and Canadian George Auld at his tenor saxophone. Yes, two veteran tenors playing together. It was fabulous. Ben's sound was truly his own, and even today, you can easily identify his recorded work. The alternating tenors were unusual and I won't forget this set.

Despite these amazing performances, the first of what would be two riots in Newport was about to take place. And it would not only ruin this concert and the weekend, but it would begin to cause major havoc to the future of the Newport annual festivals. The city fathers would take away the festival's license. The 1961 festival may not have its chance to take place.

Chapter 18
The 1960 Newport Jazz Festival
Riot at the Festival

I was privy to one of the greatest performances ever held. It was not scheduled as such.

The fabulous Oscar Peterson Trio featuring Oscar on ivories, Herb Ellis on guitar, and Ray Brown on bass were to end the show. It was to be a normal twenty minute performance. It was about 10:30 p.m. and the festival was to end at 11 p.m., according to schedule.

George Wein addressed the audience and said there was "trouble" outside, and that the gates had been broken. He asked that people consider leaving the site carefully, as soon as possible.

I spotted Louis and Elaine Lorillard leaving their front row box. I decided to take their vacant seat which was adjoining the stage. Little did I know that Oscar and his musicians would continue playing through the outside riot until 2:30 a.m., well into the wee hours of the morning.

The band played every conceivable tune that they had either made famous or recorded. They even reached for contemporary works that they had probably never even played before.

I began feeding them my own requests, which included compositions far away from their normal repertoire. Oscar even broke into a classical spectacular showing off his extended classical training background. I was truly in jazz heaven.

I went away with an infusion for this art form never to be equaled.

Aside from the riot, my three dollars for the ticket had been well spent.

My views on the riots that occurred at the Newport Festivals differ from those written by Producer George Wein, as well as the words of the Newport City Council.

At the 1960 festival, I spoke with many of the young arrivals who spoke of their frustrations. It proved that Newport was not prepared for such a turnout.

They mentioned the advertisements that were placed all across America, and how they encouraged individuals to come. There was no mention in those ads about scarcity of tickets or warnings of limited available lodging.

Individuals were expecting tickets and there were none available -- the festival was sold out.

In addition, all the lodging had been taken. People slept in their vehicles, in the streets, at the beaches and on lawns.

There were few rest rooms, so they urinated on lawns and in the streets, in telephone booths, or wherever.

There were few trash cans, so they littered the streets and private properties.

And there were not enough police. The Army National Guard and the local Naval Base Shore Patrol were called out to assist.

Alcohol and drugs also came into the picture right away. But it was the combination of the ticket shortage and a lack of housing that created the biggest problems. It led to altercations throughout the city, and at the festival ticket office, and eventually at the gates of the events themselves.

Although festival security did their best, it was not equipped to hold back the enormous crowd that had gathered outside the event. Soon the gates tumbled and the festival had to come to an abrupt, abbreviated ending.

The festival was blamed and suffered dearly, but the City of Newport must share in that awful experience. The city was truly not prepared. And after a second riot in 1971, the festival was denied renewal for future events.

In 1972 George Wein was forced to redirect his focus to New York City.

But like General Douglas McArthur returning to the Philippines, George Wein would return to Newport in the summer of 1981.

Chapter 19
From U. S. Army to Greater Boston

Fresh off my tour of duty in the Army, I moved to Boston. I would spend several years of my young life in Greater Boston.

I gained excellent employment with the Eutectic Corporation, an international Swiss firm, with headquarters in Flushing, New York. I was to manage their New England regional warehouse.

I was now poised to spread my love for jazz over all of Southern New England.

In Worcester, Massachusetts, I located Jimmy Porcella and Carol Sloane. Jimmy had a remarkable voice and was a terrific near-clone of the crooner, Mel Torme.

I followed Jimmy for years, present at many of his long-time gigs including a notable one at The Ritz-Carlton Hotel in Boston.

Carol Sloane possesses one of the finest voices in New England. Her recordings sound similar to that of the great Ella Fitzgerald. She was to perform at the 1962 Newport Festival with the great Coleman Hawkins contributing on tenor, and Bill Rubenstein at the keyboard.

Later, back in Newport, I tried to bring Jimmy and Carol together for a special performance of the music of Mel and Ella. Unfortunately it didn't work out, and the program had to be cancelled. But my effort was genuine.

Chapter 20
A Long Walk with Jazz

Back in the early 1960s, the late Senator Robert F. Kennedy, Democrat from New York and brother to the late President John Kennedy, launched a physical fitness program encouraging the country to walk and exercise.

I was managing the Boston warehouse for the Eutectic Corporation when I decided to walk from Boston to Providence, fifty miles in one day.

The challenge included delivering a package along the way to one of my company's important customers.

I completed the walk in thirteen hours. My story and pictures made the front pages of several Boston and Providence area newspapers.

While walking, I was listening to great jazz on my battery-operated transistor radio. Jazz truly helped me endure that long walk that day.

Many of those jazz radio stations are no longer playing our music. I am thankful for the music that was available to me at that time.

Chapter 21
An Attempt to Replace Jazz

After George Wein was denied his annual license in Newport, the city's summer financial situation was dire. Many local vendors and establishments suffered.

New York promoters Sid Bernstein and John Drew applied for a different entertainment license to hopefully ease Newport's financial woes, and make themselves some quick money.

In 1961, they brought entertainers Judy Garland, Bob Hope and Rhoda Fleming to this City by the Sea. They called it "Music at Newport."

I attended each of these programs. They were unusual for this small town. The talent performed to their expectations, however, the project failed financially and then some. The producers took their losses and gave up on Newport.

It sure wasn't jazz... and many of us were still hopeful that our music would return somehow.

Chapter 22
The 1962 Newport Jazz Festival
Return to Newport

Following the 1961 sabbatical, the Newport, Rhode Island Festival returned.

Freebody Park was still the site. The least expensive seat prices had risen to three dollars and twenty cents, a twenty-cent rise and the best of the reserved seats rose to five dollars and forty cents.

The Friday evening program started with Tony Tomasso and the Jewels of Dixieland. It was different, and it was the first Dixie group to perform here. It certainly was upbeat and the fans loved it.

Although I like Dixie music, I had hoped that the producers would lean more towards big band instrumentations and the special voices that had made the art form so popular. Happily, the rest of the evening went in that direction.

The great Coleman Hawkins on tenor sax led a group including the fabulous Roy Eldridge on horn, Bill Rubenstein on piano, Jim Neves at the bass and the flashy Jo Jones on drums.

Next came Dave Brubeck with his Quartet featuring the now famous Paul Desmond on alto sax, with Joe Morello on drums and Eugene Wright at the bass.

Songstress Carmen McRae came on stage with baritone saxophonist Gerry Mulligan to play with the Brubeck group. It was terrific.

After intermission, Mulligan was to return with his own group featuring Bobby Brookmeyer on horn joined by Coleman Hawkins on reeds. And Carmen McRae returned to do a number with them.

The Harry Edison Quintet was to follow featuring the wonderful voice of Joe Williams.

Carmen McRae came back to join Joe with his quintet. Also back on stage was "The Hawk," Coleman Hawkins, and Roy Eldridge. The results were sensational to say the least.

That ended the Friday evening concert. And what an ending it was.

♫ ♫ ♫

Saturday afternoon offered two seminars. The first one discussed "The Economics of the Jazz Community," fronted by John Hammond from Columbia Records. Joe Williams and Charlie Mingus were participants.

The second one, "History of Tap Dance and Its Relationship to Jazz," was headed by Dr. Marshall Stearns, the guest columnist and noted professor at Hunter College in New York. Professional dancers, Bunny Briggs and Baby Lawrence, attended and performed their struts. It was outstanding, and I was glad that I had found the time to come to see it. Later during the evening program, they were to steal the show with their excellent dance routines.

I was now convinced that tap truly belongs with jazz and I wish there would be more of it.

The Saturday evening program began with the Gene Hull Orchestra, called the Jazz Giants. The beautiful voice of Miss Carol Sloane followed accompanied by Bill Rubinstein at piano and the great Coleman Hawkins on tenor. She sure sounded a lot like Ella Fitzgerald, and it was well received by her huge number of fans.

The Charles Mingus Sextet came next. Backing up Charlie on his bass were Booker Ervin on tenor, Richard Williams on trumpet, Charles McPherson on alto and Dannie Richmond on the sticks. Featured with this group was the piano of Toshiko Mariano.

It certainly was different, as most of Mingus' works usually were. Some of my friends liked it, and some of them didn't. I appreciated the combinations and the sounds that came from this unique performer.

Max Roach came to stage next with his quartet, supported by the voices from the "Choir of Sixteen Voices." It too was different, but following Mingus made it sound more on focus than it might have been otherwise.

Mingus and Roach returned to jam for the tap show put on by the talented Bunny Briggs and Baby Lawrence. This really stole the evening. They were truly sensational.

Ending the evening was the usual work of Louis Armstrong with his group of "All Stars" led by Trummy Young on bone, Billy Kyle at the piano, William Cronk at the bass, Danny Barcelona on drums and Joe Darensbourg at clarinet.

Louis' guest stars included Yank Lawson on the horn and J. C. Higginbotham on trombone. It was a gasser and it was a great way to end the evening.

♫ ♫ ♫

Sunday afternoon offered another seminar. Maxwell Cohen, a New York attorney, led the discussion entitled, "Religion and the Concern for Jazz." Several priests were on the panel including Father O'Connor. Reedman, Sonny Rollins, and singer Clara Ward, represented the jazz performers. The program lasted only an hour. All agreed that the religious side of jazz was indeed very important and must remain a major part of the art form.

The afternoon music program began with organist Joe Bucci performing with Eddie Stacks on tenor and Jim Hall on guitar. The organ, too, remained an important part of the jazz equation.

The Clara Ward Gospel Singers worked next. Songstress Abbey Lincoln sang with them. It was a successful happening and many in the audience were singing along with them as they performed.

The Oscar Peterson Trio was to follow with Ray Brown on the bass and Ed Thigpen on the drumsticks. Another excellent Peterson performance was delivered, as expected.

Closing the Sunday afternoon concert was the Count Basie Orchestra featuring the voice of Jimmy Rushing with Oscar Peterson and Duke Ellington each playing a role.

On Sunday evening, the presentation gave focus to a so-called Iron Curtain Jazz Group called "The Wreckers" from Warsaw, Poland. They worked hard to win over the patient ticketholders. Their program was surprisingly excellent.

The Newport Jazz All-Stars were to take stage next, led by Pee Wee Russell on the clarinet, Ruby Braff on the cornet, Marshall Brown on trombone, Joe Jones on drums, John Neves on bass and producer George Wein at the piano. The guest artist was Bud Freeman on the tenor saxophone. This All Stars combination was upbeat and fantastic.

Duke Ellington and his Orchestra were to follow, featuring the voice of Aretha Franklin. Also invited to participate was the controversial Thelonious Monk at the keyboard. The place was jumping and people were happy.

Monk performed on stage next with his own quartet featuring Charlie Rouse on tenor. He continued playing mostly upbeat music, and included original compositions.

The final performers were a singing group called Lambert, Hendricks and Bavan. They meshed quite well with the early sounds of the night, and fans responded well to their now famous repertoire.

The Newport '62 Discovery of the Year Award went to The Roland Kirk Quartet, who ended the evening and this year's concert.

It was another terrific year for jazz and for Newport as well.

Chapter 23
The 1963 Newport Jazz Festival

Thursday's portion of the festival began with the Festival House Band. And it was groovy.

Pianist Thelonius Monk took the stage, with Charlie Rouse on tenor. Monk was clearly at his best and the gig was excellent.

Then Nina Simone began to sing. The audience swooned. She was certainly quite memorable as her ballads were soulful and moving.

Next up was the Cannonball Adderley Sextet, and it literally blew us away. The Adderley brothers were movin' and groovin' to say the least.

But the evening ended with a highlight, The Stan Kenton Orchestra. Kenton's new direction, sound, and rhythm captured the evening. His unique approach to jazz stood alone -- big band sounds not heard anywhere else.

♫ ♫ ♫

Friday's performance began with a group called The Angelo DiPippo Trio. The McCoy Tyner Trio which came next blew away my sinus problem. These guys were awesome.

Several small groups were to follow. The first was The Howard McGhee Four, then The Joe Daley Trio with singer Miss Ada Lee. Maynard Ferguson's Orchestra took the stage next. Maynard hit high notes that probably blew out windows all over town. He and his powerful orchestra more than paid for the price of admission. They were absolutely sensational.

Ending the program were two quartets, Dizzy Gillespie's group followed by Gerry Mulligan's. The veteran Joe Williams sang with them both. It was improvisation at its best. The place was swinging and of course, I was swinging right along with them.

What a way to end an evening. Joe's voice stayed with me for hours.

Duke Ellington

♫ ♫ ♫

Saturday's concert began with George Wein leading his Newport Jazz All-Stars. Once again, they were without sheet music and it was to feature entirely improvisation from within. They were dynamite.

I remember spilling a cola on the guy sitting next to me. A few minutes later he returned with two colas saying, "One is for you to spill if you need to, and the other is for you to enjoy." He was a swell guy. Later, I bought him a hot dog.

The Ramsey Lewis Trio followed. Lewis' piano playing was quite contemporary but very well received by the audience. I liked it so much that I bought his latest album the following day.

But it was Miss Nancy Wilson who was to steal most of the evening with her perfect pitch and romantic singing. Backed by the Sonny Rollins Quartet, she sweetened the music like only a few can do.

The evening ended with The Duke Ellington Orchestra. As usual, he and his talented musicians played all the famous numbers that had made their reputation around the world.

It was a great way to end the program. We all went away with the Ellington music fresh in our memories.

♫ ♫ ♫

Sunday's performance began with The Westwood, Massachusetts High School Dance Band. These talented youngsters more than proved themselves on the big stage. Many of the performers would have no doubt fit right in with the big bands of the day.

The Herbie Mann Sextet came next, and brought some new sounds, new compositions and plenty of pleasing music to the festival. They captured the attention of the audience, and the audience applauded with enthusiasm.

Songstress Miss Dakota Staton followed. *Darn that Dream* and several other songs swept us away. Her approach was quite different from other singers -- she was loud. You didn't miss a word. And her fans were everywhere.

Once again, Dave Brubeck appeared. Of course, Paul Desmond was on alto, with Joe Morello on drums and Eugene Wright on bass. They played their famous numbers to the delight of the upbeat audience.

The organ delights of the great Jimmy Smith then filled the stage. He, too, played tunes that he had made popular through the years, and I continued to believe that the organ truly belongs in the jazz identity.

The John Coltrane Quartet was to end the evening and the annual event. Pianist McCoy Tyner accompanied, with Eric Dolphy at alto, Jimmy Garrison on double bass and the fabulous Roy Haynes on drums.

Coltrane had yet to turn full cycle. He led several American Song Book tunes that night and put a lot of improvisational mix into his numbers. It was a great ending to 1963 at Newport.

Chapter 24
The Music Begins to Change

From the beginning, jazz has been made up of many individual contributions. Different beats, rhythms, sounds and styles have always confused its overall identity. People have always had difficulty labeling it: *What is jazz, and what isn't?*

To make it even more difficult, the 1960's brought huge changes in the music, and quickly, the sounds and performances changed. As an outsider looking in, I recognized that many of the top performers had started to mix more improvisational freedoms into their performances.

Louis Armstrong had given them that permission, so to speak, and more individuals were now even adding scat, and other unusual improvisational techniques.

Miles Davis, John Coltrane, Ornette Coleman and others began going in different directions. Some of their sounds became unrecognizable, lacking the sweet melodies we had all grown accustomed to.

The emotional sounds from jazz's roots in the slavery era, were still there, but with new influence. The classical training that some had received began to surface. New groups were being formed and classical performances became more frequent. Solos became less defined and individualistic. Many of these solos were so different that they could never be repeated.

Around this time, I made a New York City visit with a group of friends. We visited the famous Basin Street East where reedman Gerry Mulligan was playing with drummer Chico Hamilton. The whole evening featured music I had never heard. Mulligan reached deep to perform new compositions that he had written. Some were, "way out."

His group performed well, but I left that night without hearing any familiar works. I began to re-evaluate this new jazz approach.

The Newport Jazz Festival planning committee was re-evaluating the performing talent at festivals, too.

Change had always been a part of jazz. For example, the 1958 Newport concert had gone to four days, and Mahalia Jackson captured the audience with beautiful gospel. I remember stamping my feet and clapping to the rhythm that she presented. It was truly a breathtaking experience.

Miles Davis on horn and Thelonious Monk at the piano led The Miles Davis Sextet that crossed normal jazz lines to create new sounds. It was hard to evaluate at times, but it was indeed jazz.

And it was at this time that the movie, *Jazz on a Summer's Day* was filmed and released. The movie became the first visual promotion connecting jazz to Newport, and of course, directly to the festivals. Unfortunately, George Wein's name and deserving credits were omitted by the film producers. But my friends and I still enjoyed the film, the music, and the many stories that came from its contents.

At about this time, I had graduated high school and was attending Providence College in a pre-medical program. An occasional musical gig, at the request of the union, kept me close to this ever-changing jazz landscape.

I learned Dizzy Gillespie had come to town with a small group and was to perform at Rhode Island College. I arrived early and watched them set-up. Dizzy was loosening his trumpet valves. I approached him, and asked him what he was using for valve oil.

He turned around and said, "Here Dude, you can have this bottle." He handed me a bottle that was about half-full and said, "Don't think the oil is going to get you to play any better."

I thanked him. He gave me a high five. I asked him to play *Night in Tunisia*. He responded, "That goes without saying!"

That night he mentioned my request and played it. He asked me to stand up and wave to the audience. I was embarrassed, but won't forget the moment, nor will I forget Dizzy's spectacular performance.

Chapter 25
Accepting the Changing of Jazz

Although a generation of jazz followers have passed on, there is still a new, existing market today.

Those of us who have favored the more traditional music of the mid Twentieth Century hang on diligently to the occasional sounds of that era's music, whether through the surviving veterans or through the few new talents who choose to rekindle some of the favorite music of that successful era of jazz growth.

Today's music is quite different, to say the least. It has passed through major changes, with new style, sounds, depth of sounds, rhythms and crossovers. It has forged new boundaries and new elements of tone, reaching to higher physiological meaning, and creating music beyond the simple romantic objectives of the previous generation's music.

The older generation struggles at the eardrums with the loss of real melody in the new compositions. Repetitious beating sometimes becomes annoying and objectionable. Adjustments have not come easily. Many of the older generation have not yet accepted these differences. Some keep trying.

Jazz's acceptance of bebop, fusion and others took a while. Funky sounds and rap are still enduring their trials now.

Once again, jazz will be moving in new directions, just as it has in the past.

Chapter 26
The 1964 Newport Jazz Festival
The Last at Freebody Park

The 1964 Newport Jazz Festival featured a memorable segment fronted by the Stan Getz Quartet. Beside Getz's wonderful saxophone, Gary Burton on vibes contributed great variety to the gig.

Also with the Getz group came the voice of Astrud Gilberto, fresh from Brazil. The album they produced together had become a favorite in the jazz world. Amazingly, the flugelhorn of Chet Baker was added to this gathering.

And wailing they went. When some of us think of Getz today, it is this performance with Astrud that always comes to mind.

Some stride music was purposely put into the program when the festival brought in Joe Sullivan from Chicago, a stride pianist. Included in his performance were Bud Freeman, Peanuts Hucko and Max Kaminsky. The reeds blended in so well they actually took center focus.

Next, drummer Max Roach worked with Eddie Kohn on bass, Clifford Jordan on tenor and Lonnie Smith at the keyboard. Joining them was the voice of Abbey Lincoln.

Then, Ben Webster used his saxophone to jam with Buck Clayton on horn, Al Grey on bone, Slam Stewart on bass and Sir Charles Thompson on the sticks.

Following them was the sweet vibrato voice of Sarah Vaughan which rang throughout the park. She captured all the attention, and rightfully so. Only Sarah could slur and embrace the key lyrics of the American Song Book. Her performance was breathtaking.

And once again, Dave Brubeck was asked to finish off the festival. His *Pennies from Heaven* was just wonderful. Many, many fans stood to cheer. The Quartet deserved these exuberant final bows. It was a meaningful ending to a great show.

Chapter 27
The 1965 Newport Jazz Festival

The 1965 festival's Thursday evening performance brought
Memphis Slim with his piano and Willie Dixon on bass to the
stage. I thought they belonged at the Newport Folk Festival instead, but obviously management thought otherwise.

Peter Seeger followed with his guitar. I enjoyed his performance, but again, believed he belonged at the folk festival, too.

Finally, Max Kaminsky came out with his horn followed by Bud
Freeman on tenor, Morey Field at the drums, Jack Lesberg on
bass and the producer himself George Wein at the piano. It was
a new group of All-Stars fronted by Wein. And as expected,
they were excellent.

Next up came the Muddy Waters Blues Band featuring Otis Spann at the piano, James Cotton at the harmonica and Little Bo at tenor. Once again, I enjoyed the music but felt they, too, belonged at the folk festival, not here.

Dizzy Gillespie was to perform next. His trumpet was accompanied by James Moody on alto saxophone, Chris White on bass, Rudy Collins at the drums and Kenny Barron at the keyboard. There was a lot of noise and it was great. These guys sure pushed hard at the melody and the fans loved it.

The Les McCann Trio and the Modern Jazz Quartet followed, and Joe Williams added his wonderful voice to the mix. The performance ended the Thursday night event.

♫ ♫ ♫

Friday afternoon's line-up opened with The Jazz Composer's Orchestra, directed by Mike Mantler and Carla Bley, and a group of others. The music didn't make it with me. They were musically somewhere else. But I guess to many, it was jazz.

The Archie Shepp Trio followed and filled in the rough edges left behind by the last group. These musicians were upbeat and well accepted by the crowd.

The Paul Bley Quartet performed next. I was away from my seat when they went on stage. The Cecil Taylor Group followed them. Cecil was a pianist and poet with classical jazz background, and his work at the keyboard showed it. Even his style had found a place in the jazz midstream. He ended the afternoon session.

Friday evening began with the upbeat sounds of The Art Blakey Quintet featuring Gary Bartz at the alto, John Gilmore on tenor, Lee Morgan on trumpet and John Hicks at the keyboard. It was a gasser.

Then popular singer, Miss Carmen McRae came on stage with Norman Simmons at the piano. Her voice was on high. Romance was everywhere. Her performance dazzled a lot of people. I was in heaven.

The Miles Davis Group followed her featuring Wayne Shorter on tenor, Herbie Hancock at the piano, Ron Carter at bass and Tony Williams at the drums. It was a sensational performance, and the whole place was rockin'.

After intermission, Thelonious Monk brought his group to the stage. Accompanying his piano were Charlie Rouse at tenor, Ben Riley at the drums and Larry Gales at bass. They blended perfectly. It was a great set.

John Coltrane arrived with his tenor saxophone to end the evening. Also performing were Elvin Jones on drums, Jim Garrison on bass and McCoy Tyner at the keys. These veterans created wonderful music, yet the melodies were being hidden behind their wild improvisations. It was a different way to end the Friday evening program. Even the weather was unsettled.

♫ ♫ ♫

Saturday afternoon's programming featured a drum workshop with masters Louis Bellson, Art Blakey, Roy Haynes, Elvin Jones, Jo Jones, Joe Morello and, to top it off, the great Buddy Rich.

Needless to say sticks were flyin' -- and tempos got way out-of-hand. As expected, each artist had his own style of thumping, and each got the applause they truly deserved. It was amazing to see most of the great drummers of the times in one performance in one event. I won't forget it. It had to be one for the jazz history books.

Saturday evening began with a jam session that featured Toshiko at the keyboard with Sonny Stitt and Illinois Jacquet on saxophones, Tony Scott on clarinet, Howard McGhee on horn and Buddy Rich on the sticks. Wow! It was indeed memorable. The fires had been lit.

From Japan came the voice of Miss Mieko Hirota accompanied by Billy Taylor at the keyboard with Grady Tate on drums. There was no melody.

Then it was time for the Dave Brubeck Quartet with Paul Desmond on alto, Joe Morello on drums, Eugene Wright on the bass and Dave Brubeck on the keys. They did their usual famous tunes and a few new ones. The crowd loved *Take Five* which by now had become their best known number.

The Herbie Mann Octet featured Herbie on flute, Dave Pike on vibes, Jane Getz on piano, Jack Hitchcock on trombone and others. It was soft and romantic with a different rhythm. And most of the fans loved it.

Next, Earl "Fatha" Hines captured the audience with his piano recital. His orthodox renditions of traditional song numbers caught everyone's attention. He was a true old school entertainer.

The Duke Ellington Orchestra ended the evening, with veteran Louis Bellson featured on drums. Their rhythm was upbeat. Many people danced in the back of the crowd.

It was another great Saturday evening concert well worth the ticket.

♫ ♫ ♫

The Sunday afternoon show started with the Denny Zeitlin Trio featuring Charlie Haden on bass and Jerry Granelli on the sticks. It was a good choice for the opener. They were groovin' with plenty of melody.

Next was the guitar master Wes Montgomery's Trio with Wynton Kelly at the keyboard, Paul Chambers at the bass and Jimmy Cobb on the drums. Wes was truly one of the finest jazz guitar players anywhere, and didn't disappoint us.

Two other groups followed. One was from South Africa and their music was not received particularly well. It was pure African rhythm and beat without melody.

Finishing the Sunday afternoon gig was the Stan Getz Quintet. Getz's saxophone put polish on many famous numbers. Only Getz's sweet tone could have performed these compositions with such perfection. It represented a wonderful ending to a great afternoon.

Sunday evening was to be a thriller, too. Oscar Peterson's trio featuring Herb Ellis on guitar and Ray Brown on bass were used as a set-up for what was to come. Their performance included perfection on several standard songs that brought the audience to their feet.

The Count Basie Orchestra took the stage and broke into swing for a couple of numbers.

And then! A helicopter suddenly appeared in the sky and landed on the field, and out jumped Frank Sinatra. Frank was to spend a full hour singing with the Basie Band behind him. It was spectacular. His voice was full of excitement as he punched out song after song, one right after another. Many were well known tunes that he had made famous over his long career.

Frank appeared happy and thrilled to be in Newport with the Basie Group. He even sang to the Count himself with the Count finishing it on piano.

That hour went by so quickly that it seemed like only a few minutes.

Sinatra gave us our money's worth and then some. I will never forget his strong delivery, his upbeat presentation and the respect he had for Newport and the fans that had packed the place to hear and see him that night.

Today it stands among the finest moments in Newport's storied music history.

What an ending to a long and fruitful jazz weekend.

Chapter 28
Enjoying the Boston Jazz Scene

In the 1960's I went to school in Boston -- Bentley Accounting at night and MIT during the day -- supporting my family in between. I worked and studied, and used music as my diversion.

While there, I became privy to a Boston jazz explosion. I discovered that many wonderful clubs and groups were available in the city.

The Berklee School of Music was at the time producing many of the future stars in jazz. Among the talents coming out of this school over the coming decades were Diana Krall, Rebecca Parris, Gray Sargent, Marshall Wood, Gary Johnson, Debra Mann, Matthew Quinn, Wynton Marsalis and his brother Branford, and many, many others.

The local venues featured most of them, and it was quite easy to find good music pretty much anywhere in Greater Boston.

I had the good fortune to see and hear this talent developing right before me. It became an unforgettable period in my jazz life.

Ted Casher

Today, the jazz scene is more difficult to find in the Boston area, yet new and brilliant musicians continue to flow from Berklee, the New England Conservatory of Music, and other excellent Greater Boston university musical programs.

A long list of these Boston-educated performers have played and continue to play the Newport stage.

Burt Jagolinzer

It was easy to find many wonderful female singers in the area, too. Highlighting this group were the special talents of Rebecca Parris, Donna Burns, Amanda Carr and Shawnn Monteiro.

Reed players from the city included the talented Ted Casher, Dick Johnson and Greg Abate.

Ted Casher, a Harvard graduate, became the consummate accompanying man in Boston and in the north country. Even in advancing age, he is still among the finest reedmen in New England, still playing better than ever.

The late Dick Johnson and the late trumpet great Lou Colombo seemed to be everywhere performing at special events, celebrations and in select jazz clubs. Their music and presentations made wonderful memories.

Gray Sargent, playing his trusty guitar, and Marshall Wood on stand-up bass, paid their dues locally and now tour and perform with the great Tony Bennett.

Debra Mann, today, teaches piano and performs cabaret throughout Southern New England.

Gary Johnson, son of the late Dick Johnson, is one of New England's most sought after veteran drummers.

Tim Ray plays piano with the best. His movement on the keys is spectacular. He shows up most anywhere. He has also played with many of the great performers in jazz.

And Greg Abate is now one of the leading reedmen in the world. He paid his dues locally in these early days and now he is an international performer. We who listened to him in the early years are proud of his rise to fame, and believe he truly deserves all the recognition that has come with it.

It was a very special time for local talent and their performances. And I was privileged to be there during that period. Their representation of the American Songbook and traditional jazz was alive and could be found in most of New England.

Chapter 29
While Searching for Jazz in Boston

Lennie's on The Turnpike in Danvers, Massachusetts, often hired the world-renown drummer, Buddy Rich, and his spirited orchestra.

I loved Buddy's upbeat arrangements, many of which had never been heard before. Usually, they featured loud trumpets at high octaves and Buddy's slick soloing. He had been known to have, "fast hands and a heavy right foot."

I would go away from those shows charged with a jazz rhythm that would stay with me for days. That infusion was truly a side of jazz that helped define the art form on a high-quality note.

'Round Newport

At the Bedford, Massachusetts Stouffer Hotel, you could usually find a modern singing group called Puttin' on the Ritz led by Darryl Bosteels and Sharon Harris. They played solo with just a bass backup named Les Harris, Jr. Their sound resembled Manhattan Transfer and the Four Freshmen. They were awesome. I enjoyed their performances many times over the years.

Back in the late 1990's I met Thelonious Monk, Jr., then an established veteran drummer, performing at The Charles Hotel in Cambridge, Massachusetts.

During his intermission, I told him about spending some special time with his late father in the earliest years of the Newport festivals.

During one of the afternoon festival seminars, I sat next to his father when Anita O'Day was delivering a speech about scat singing and the importance of the swing-era in which she had participated.

I remember Monk saying to me, "for a white women, she is groovy and scats quite well."

I spilled some of my cola on his shoes and immediately apologized for the embarrassing mistake. He responded, "If I had my shoe brush with me I'd make the most of it... with a great shine."

Junior was very interested in my story about his dad and he thanked me for taking the time to relate it to him.

I also met the eclectic jazz singer, Mark Murphy, several times. In the late 1990's, he was performing at the Charles Hotel in Cambridge with the talented gifted singer, Rebecca Parris. They were quite a team.

Becky dissected Cole Porter's *Dancing-in-the-Dark* tune. Mark took it an octave higher and added some original scat and wild improvisation. They ended the piece with a flurry of discords that worked in a strange but beautiful way. If Cole Porter had been present, he would have been amazed.

Their relationship, though fragile at the time, was an indelible example of the new direction in the changing jazz world.

I won't forget those special performances.

Chapter 30
The 1966 Newport Jazz Festival

Friday evening opened with the Florida Jazz Quintet followed by the return of the now famous Newport Jazz Festival All-Stars directed by George Wein at the piano, with Ruby Braff on the horn, Bud Freeman on tenor and Gerry Mulligan on baritone sax.

They were excellent as usual, performed without sheet music and were loaded with improvisation.

The Dave Brubeck Quartet performed next. Once again they opened with the famous numbers that had run the charts. And once again *Take Five* highlighted their program. We all loved it.

Organ playing took the stage next as the great Jimmy Smith began his important set. It was an excellent choice after Brubeck, and it settled down the audience that had reached a high during the last group's performance. Miss Esther Phillips' voice joined Jimmy Smith's organ, and the fans loved it.

The Archie Shepp Quartet finished the evening. Archie played the saxophone, sang, and played the piano with Roswell Rudd on the bone. I hung around until the end and I was not disappointed. These guys made music and super jazz. The other members of his quartet included Willie Harris on drums, Charlie Haden on bass and Howard Johnson on the tuba.

♫ ♫ ♫

The Saturday afternoon program featured four groups.

The opening act was the Bill Dixon Quartet with dancer Judith Dunn. I'm not sure if this gang should have been here. The interplay between the dancing and the music didn't jive.

Next up was The Charles Lloyd Quartet with Charles on tenor and flute, Jack DeJohnette on drums, Cecil McBee at the bass and Keith Jarrett at the piano. They made super jazz music.

The Horace Silver Quintet featured Horace at the keyboard, with Roger Humphries on the drums, Larry Ridley on bass,

Woody Shaw on horn and Tyrone Washington on tenor sax. This was a great set proving Horace Silver's justified fame.

The John Coltrane Quintet followed Horace featuring John on the tenor, Rashid Ali on drums, Jimmy Garrison on bass, Alice McCleod at the piano and Farrell Sanders on tenor sax. It was clear Coltrane's music had begun to change, and had become outrageously improvisational. Not everyone in the audience took to it.

The Saturday evening concert began with the Charlie Byrd Trio starring Charlie at the guitar, with Gene Byrd at the bass and Bill Reichenbach on drums. Byrd's classical jazz performance was sensational. He is truly one of the few masters of the jazz guitar.

Songstress Nina Simone performed romantic ballads next with her own group, including Rudy Stevenson on guitar and flute, Robbie Hamilton on drums and Lyle Atkinson on the bass.

Stan Getz followed with a Quartet featuring Stan at tenor, Roy Haynes on drums, Steve Swallow on bass and Gary Burton on vibes. How could anyone not like the Getz sound and his talented accompaniments?

Monk was next. Thelonious was at his best at the piano, with Larry Gales at the bass, Ben Riley at the drums and Charlie Rouse at tenor. They were smokin' hot and the crowd appreciated it.

The Mel Lewis-Thad Jones Orchestra went on with Bobby Brookmeyer on trombone and Hank Jones at the piano. This nineteen piece group blew us apart. Their arrangements were special and they woke up the audience with their magnitude.

And finally, the fabulous voice of Joe Williams came to the stage to help conclude this wonderful Saturday evening program.

♫ ♫ ♫

The Sunday afternoon event featured the Al Cohn-Zoot Sims Quartet. They settled people into their seats. This reed combo was about to entertain and entertain they did. If there was a complaint, the set was too short. The audience wanted more.

The Woody Herman Orchestra was to complete the afternoon program. The big band included Woody on his trusty clarinet, supplemented by Stan Getz, Al Cohn, Zoot Sims and Gerry Mulligan. What a smash. They literally rocked the place.

Wow!

Sunday evening's program began with a special group consisting of the great Teddy Wilson on the keys, with Coleman Hawkins on tenor and the trumpets of Clark Terry. They were awesome with upbeat tempos that got the audience pounding.

The evening closed with The Duke Ellington Orchestra blasting its way through their many famous hits and closing with tunes from the voice of the great Ella Fitzgerald. I was once again in heaven. Ella was still at the top of her game giving the audience everything she had. We responded by standing and clapping throughout her performance. I won't forget this moment.

♫ ♫ ♫

Monday afternoon offered two workshops, both conducted by Dr. Billy Taylor. The first was a guitar program that included Charlie Byrd, Kenny Burrell, Grant Green and Attila Zoller. The second was a trumpet program that included Dizzy Gillespie, Bobby Hackett, Thad Jones, Howard McGhee, Ruby Braff, Kenny Dorham, Clark Terry and Carl Warwick.

These seminars were wonderful. Not only did they give the masters a chance to converse and exchange information, but they gave the attendees like me a chance to meet these talents directly and compare their methods in one big sweep.

The Monday evening program began with The Miles Davis Quintet. Miles had Ron Carter on bass, Herbie Hancock on the keys, Wayne Shorter on tenor and Tony Williams on the drums. As usual, they made a lot of noise mixed with some melody to the beat for the watching and listening audience. It was cool.

The Herbie Mann Septet and Dizzy's quintet were to follow. They continued the theme of mostly upbeat tunes. It was getting to be a very upbeat night.

The Count Basie Orchestra was to finish off the evening and the weekend. Jimmy Rushing sang and Basie did his thing at the piano to end this great event.

The 1966 festival had come to an end and the Basie music was a fitting closure.

Chapter 31
The 1967 Newport Jazz Festival

The Friday evening 1967 Newport festival began with the African sounds of Olatunji and Company. Their sounds were new to me, and it was the first of this type to be performed in Newport. I thought the rhythm was great, but it lacked the melodic tones that attracted me to jazz.

Next came Earl "Fatha" Hines featuring the horn of Roy Eldridge. This was more like it. They played familiar numbers and the audience received them with snapping fingers and a lot of clapping hands.

Next, George Wein and his Newport Jazz Festival All-Stars kept us all upbeat. They played several of the standards of the past without sheet music. In this group were reedmen Pee Wee Russell on the licorice-stick and Bud Freeman on tenor, with Ruby Braff on horn, Jack Lesberg on the bass and Don Lamond on drums. And added to the group was the complete rhythm section of the Count Basie Orchestra.

It was a terrific happening, with plenty of great music.

After intermission, the Count Basie Orchestra took over, and they featured the voice of Joe Williams once again at his best. Basie's most famous recorded numbers filled the festival as usual, and it quickly became the high of the evening.

The "Birth of Bop" followed with the performance of Dizzy Gillespie on his bent horn, Thelonious Monk on keys and Max Roach on sticks. Their bop was well accepted by the listeners and some dancing even took place in the aisles.

The evening ended with the work of The Modern Jazz Quartet. As usual, it featured Percy Heath on bass, John Lewis at the piano, with Milt Jackson on vibes and Connie Kay at the drums.

Saturday evening's program began with the music of Gary Burton on vibes with Larry Coryell on his guitar. Then Dizzy performed again with a different quartet. It was slick, featuring many melodies from the American Song Book.

Earl "Fatha" Hines at the piano then gave us his usual work, accenting many old and memorable tunes.

Next came the beautiful and haunting voice of Nina Simone and her trio. Nina was at the peak of her career and she sang many of the numbers that had made her success. It was wonderfully performed.

After intermission, the John Handy Quintet took stage. It featured John on alto saxophone, with the violin of Michael White, Freddie Redd at the piano, Jerry Hahn on guitar and Terry Clarke on the drums. Their work was cool. They were new to me and I enjoyed their presentation.

The Herbie Mann Sextet followed with Herbie on flute and a group of gifted percussionists. Though it was different, it was well received by their fans.

Closing the evening was The Buddy Rich Orchestra. The audience came to their feet quickly when Buddy led the very first upbeat number. Other great arrangements followed throughout the set.

It became a smart way to end the evening. The music stayed with me all the way home.

♫ ♫ ♫

Sunday afternoon produced a saxophone workshop featuring Booker Ervin, followed by a vibes workshop with Milt Jackson,

Gary Burton, Lionel Hampton, Red Norvo and a few others. It was very worthwhile and memorable.

Sunday evening's musical program began with the Blues Project, then featuring the voice of Marilyn Maye.

And finally, the Miles Davis Quintet took stage. Miles' horn was accompanied by Wayne Shorter on sax, Tony Williams on drums and Herbie Hancock on the keyboard. It was a blast.

After intermission came the Max Roach Quintet and the Bill Evans Trio.

The evening finished with the Woody Herman Orchestra featuring Woody on his trusty clarinet.

It too was a great way to end the program. The big orchestra sound stayed with me the rest of the evening.

♫ ♫ ♫

The Monday program included an afternoon session led by the Milford, Massachusetts Youth Band under the direction of veteran saxophonist Boots Mussulli. They were spectacular. The arrangements and solos were especially outstanding.

The Don Ellis Orchestra from California completed the afternoon event. Ellis's trumpet and big-band members blew us away. They had some special arrangements and improvisations that truly documented the orchestra's west coast successes.

Monday evening's program began with the return of the Milford, Massachusetts Youth Band. They sure sounded terrific and drew the welcoming audience's immediate attention.

Illinois Jacquet performed his sensational saxophone with organist and pianist, Milt Buckner. They, too, were dynamite.

And next were vibraphonist Red Norvo's All Stars with drummer Don Lamond and double-bassist Jack Lesberg. They played famous numbers and were well received.

The Dave Brubeck Quartet followed with their usual upbeat gig featuring Paul Desmond on sax with their famous tunes. Many in the audience had come just to hear this group.

Sarah Vaughan took stage with her trio. She swooned us with her melodic emotion and slurs. Only Sarah could bring chills to your body with the touches of improvisation she shared throughout her performance. Being a Sarah fan, I was in heaven.

After intermission came the Wes Montgomery Trio. His superior guitar playing always stands out. He was at the peak of his career and enchanted the audience with wonderful renditions of many famous American standards.

The evening and weekend were to end with the Lionel Hampton Alumni Orchestra featuring Joe Newman, Herb Pomeroy and Snooky Young on trumpets, Al Grey, Garnett Brown and Benny Powell on trombones, Frank Foster, Dave Young and Jerome Richardson on reeds, William Mackel on guitar, Steve Little on drums, John Spruill on piano and of course Lionel on vibes.

It was loud and demonstrative. People clapped and cheered. We all left our seats well entertained and happy, the music imbedded in us as we all drove home.

Chapter 32
Collecting Jazz Albums

I had been collecting jazz albums for about 30 years. They were purchased from flea markets, yards sales or tag sales around New England. My brother Ken contributed his bunch to my collection as well.

Before long I had amassed approximately four thousand records, of which three thousand were assorted jazz. The remaining collection consisted of R&B, some country-western and even a good number of classical albums.

Many of the jazz records originated from the earliest days of studio work. They included some of jazz history's most important performers. About a dozen of them were personally autographed. It was a collector's dream.

Unfortunately, I had to sell the collection because of a family move. It had grown too big to fit into our new place. A local medical doctor stole the lot, figuratively speaking.

Today that collection would easily be valued at more than five times what that good doctor paid for it.

Chapter 33
The 1968 Newport Jazz Festival

The popular and talented singer Dionne Warwick was the featured act at the 1968 festival. Her alliance with pianist and composer Burt Bacharach had taken the music world by storm. At
the time of her performance in Newport, they had three top hits
that could be heard everywhere. She was to maintain her popularity from the 1960's and into the seventies and beyond.

Festival management wisely used her likeness in their annual
advertising. She sold out the place. You couldn't find a ticket
anywhere. She and Bacharach had become the rage.

True to expectations, they were excellent, performing not only their world-famous hits but adding a series of new songs.

Their scheduled time slot seemed too short. The audience clearly wanted more.

Among the other performers who helped make the 1968 festival memorable included the fabulous Wes Montgomery on guitar. His deliveries of hand-picked tunes were sensational.

Others featured that year included the multiple-horns of Clark Terry and the trumpet of Warren Vache.

Al Grey's outstanding performance on his trombone was a standout, as well, as was Flip Phillips' performance on the reeds and Kenny Washington on the drums that helped end this year's program.

Like all of the previous festivals, it too was terrific.

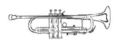

Chapter 34
The 1969 Newport Jazz Festival

Grammy Award winning guitarist and singer George Benson was to lead off the 1969 event. George had recorded with the Count Basie Orchestra and Benny Goodman's Band. He had worked at the Playboy Jazz Festival and had been discovered by producer, John Hammond.

But he was at his finest performing here at Newport.

The rest of the festival that year included sensational presentations by the great composer and pianist, Bill Evans, with his famous trio of bassist Scott LaFaro and drummer Paul Motian.

Also performing was Freddie Hubbard, who blasted away on his trumpet and Phil Woods who complemented with his reeds.

Jazz songstress, Anita O'Day, got everyone's attention with her upbeat renditions from The American Songbook. Her scat blended well with several of the melodies.

The festival of 1969 was indeed another in a growing list of memorable events at Newport.

Chapter 35
Recognizing Jazz's Unusual Musical Sounds

Those of us who follow jazz closely can recognize many of the great artists just by ear.

It is quite interesting that many of the most famous performers have been able to use their instruments to create unique sounds that separate themselves from the others in their field.

No doubt Louis Armstrong's voice and trumpet will always be recognizable. But other trumpet greats have also created their own uniqueness.

Harry James's horn was always his own, developed mostly by the range and sweetness of his vibrato. Ruby Braff's cornet is certainly different, too.

Bix Beiderbecke's unique sound comes from background accompaniment that documented his early era.

As a youngster, I learned to associate instruments with talented individuals.

For example, Erroll Garner's unusual treatment of the keyboard became indelible in my musical memory. And no one imitated Miles Davis. His sounds were strikingly different to say the least. And so were Stan Getz's saxophone and Charlie Parker's saxophone sounds, too.

Count Basie's Band was not the same as the Duke Ellington Orchestra. You can easily tell them apart.

The voices of Ella Fitzgerald, Carmen McRae, Sarah Vaughan and Billie Holiday could not be mistaken. Even a novice could recognize the differences.

Jazz historians will always be able to describe the amazing special creations developed by these talented musicians. Each has found large numbers of followers, like me, who will always appreciate their unique sounds and skills.

A student of jazz can separate many of the great arrangers by their methods and by their selections of rhythm and use of instruments. Glen Gray, Billy Strayhorn, Sammy Nestico, Neal Hefti, Stan Kenton, Bill Evans and others are recognizable in this way.

Charts today have unusual riffs, not necessarily melodic. They reach far into discord land and bring out sounds from basic instruments that fracture the veteran composers' objectives.

Someone studying an instrumental score today has a more difficult route to the art of copying an admired artist's skills. It's not like it used to be.

To play with excellent groups today, you must be a great reader of your musical part. There is more competition, as new musicians are well-schooled by some of the finest musical institutions that offer gifted students a formal education in the jazz art form.

CHAPTER 36
Quality Jazz in Arizona

Mom and Dad retired to Arizona in early 1968. Each year, I would travel west to visit them.

Don and Sue Miller, owners of a Phoenix local travel agency, organized the first of their annual Paradise Valley Jazz Parties in Scottsdale.

My brother Ken introduced me to this incredible jazz happening which brought some of America's greatest musicians to Arizona for one weekend each year.

Over a twenty year span, we witnessed the dynamite performances of pianists Sir Roland Hanna, and Dave Frishberg, drummers Butch Miles, Louie Bellson, and Bobby Rosengarden, trumpet player Byron Stripling, Milt Hinton on bass, reedman Scott Hamilton, Bob Wilber, and Ricky Woodward, Al Grey on bones, Herb Ellis on guitar, and singers Joe Williams and Pug Wilber.

Byron Stripling

The setting in Scottsdale was terrific. During the "breaks" you could mingle, enjoy coffee with the talent, take personal photos and even get collectible autographs.

Ken and I developed special relationships with many of these artists. How lucky we were to be at these events and become close to these gifted quality individuals.

Burt Jagolinzer

And we cannot overlook the great job that Don and Sue Miller did during this era to bring together this talent on their limited budget. This program still exists and is held annually in the spring.

♫ ♫ ♫

Over the years jazz has been available in many different areas of Arizona. Phoenix, being the area's largest city, captured the best jazz from the west coast.

Within the greater-Phoenix domain, Nancy, my significant other, and I have been fortunate to discover the likes of pianists Danny Long and Judy Roberts plus the sensational reedman, Greg Fishman, often found at Remington's restaurant and lounge at Scottsdale Road. Their gig starts early evening and ends around 10:30 p.m. most nights. They masterfully capture the American Song Book and ramble on with a cabaret style, and some upbeat melodies, that entertain the local jazz enthusiasts.

The talented voice of Renee Patrick has haunted us in recent years. She sings like the veteran Nancy Wilson, but with easy bursts of improvisation that establishes her own identity. She is worth listening to, and could be a real find in a new jazz talent search.

We purchased her latest CD with Judy Roberts at the keys and regularly play it. It's a keeper!

The new Musical Instrument Museum in Scottsdale is truly a must see, as there is a section strictly for jazz. But their collections of instruments include items from all over the world, some instruments so rare they are nearly unheard of even to many musical collectors and professionals.

There we were, in the museum, entertained by the voice of Jane Monheit in a special evening performance full of wonderful upbeat melodies performed at her best.

Chapter 37
Finding a New Life and Direction

The late Bob Parenti and I shared a love and involvement in trumpet playing. We would meet on occasion at local jazz events and talk about horn presentations, equipment changes and new, recently discovered talent.

Unfortunately, the doctors found cancer throughout his body and his life quickly came to a tragic end.

His widow, Nancy, and I came together through jazz and our jazz friends. We found a common love for dancing and the music. We owe this important connection to the encouragement of our dear friend, Dinah Baker, and others.

Today, Nancy and I spend much of our time traveling and con-
stantly looking for good jazz. It is our real passion and we love
it.

Chapter 38
The 1970 Newport Jazz Festival

The program on Friday, July 10, 1970 began with the sponsor's salute to Louis Armstrong. The Schlitz Beer Company, the event's sponsor, had become an important catch for George Wein.

The Eureka Brass Band from New Orleans took the stage next and pounded away with some Dixie that got everyone's attention.

Next was the Bobby Hackett Quintet featuring Bobby on his special horn. He was accompanied by Dave McKenna at the keys, Benny Morton on the bone, Jack Lesberg on bass and Cliff Leeman at the drums. It was wonderful.

Then The New Orleans Classic Ragtime Band took stage. William Russell was on violin, Lionel Ferbos on trumpet, Orange Kellin at clarinet, Paul Crawford on trombone, Cie Frazier at the drums, James Prevost on bass and the leader, Lars Edegran, at the keyboard. It was cool and the fans loved it.

A Trumpet Choir followed featuring the spectacular horns of Dizzy Gillespie, Bobby Hackett, Joe Newman, Wild-Bill Davison, Ray Nance and Jimmy Owens. They were supported by Dave McKenna at the piano, Larry Ridley at bass and Lenny McBrowne at the drums. It was loud and colorful with upbeat sounds that delighted everyone. Wow.

After intermission, the New Orleans Preservation Hall Jazz Band entertained. The great Mahalia Jackson followed, accompanied by flute, piano and organ. There were tears in everyone's eyes. Her blending of religion and blues is incomparable.

Louis Armstrong had to follow Mahalia. He performed with Dave McKenna on the piano, Larry Ridley on the bass and Lenny McBrowne on the drums. And then everyone came back on stage to finish the evening. It was truly a gas.

♫ ♫ ♫

Saturday's activities began with three workshops. The violin workshop featured Ray Nance, Mike White and Jean-Luc Ponty.

The drum workshop included performances from Chico Hamilton, Elvin Jones, Philippe Joe Jones and Jonathan (Jo) Jones. There was also a trumpet workshop featuring Dizzy Gillespie, Joe Newman and Jimmy Owens. Performances followed. It was a great afternoon.

Saturday evening's line-up began with the Kenny Burrell Trio, featuring Kenny on guitar, Larry Ridley on the bass and Lenny McBrowne on drums.

Next to perform were the reeds of Dexter Gordon. His sound was easily identifiable. He was a fabulous soloist.

The Dizzy Gillespie Quintet came next. Dizzy was accompanied by George Davis on guitar, Mike Longo at the keyboard, Larry Rockwell on bass and David Lee on the drums. The performance was upbeat and cool.

The Fiddlers followed featuring Jean Luc Ponty, Mike White and Ray Nance, all on violins. It was quite different and proved that violin had a place in jazz. They were excellent to watch and fun to listen to.

Nina Simone graced the evening next with wonderful selections and an inspired performance. Nina was at her best and she was well received by all.

The evening ended with the Herbie Mann Quintet featuring Herbie on his flute, followed by the Ike and Tina Turner Revue.

They were perfect closing acts for any Saturday program.

♫ ♫ ♫

Sunday afternoon featured the Roberta Flack Trio with Bernard Sweetney on drums and Terry Plumeri on the bass. Next, Comedian Bill Cosby came on stage with Badfoot Brown and the Bunions Bradford Marching Band. Although the music has changed over the years and I enjoy their talents, these two acts did not seem appropriate to begin the day's program.

Sunday evening started with the Eddie Harris Quartet featuring Eddie on tenor, with Kenny Barron at the piano, Cecil McBee on bass and Harold Jones on drums. Then the Les McCann Group followed, with Les singing and at the keyboard.

The Cannonball Adderley Quintet was next on stage with Cannonball on saxophone and brother Nat on cornet. The group was absolutely terrific.

After intermission, the Buddy Rich Orchestra crowded the stage. The full orchestra sounded spectacular. Of course Buddy's unique drum solos stole the show.

The evening and weekend ended on a high note with another exceptional performance from the great Ella Fitzgerald. She was still at the peak of her career. The fans loved it. Ella was accompanied by the Tommy Flanagan Trio, featuring Tommy at the piano, Ed Thigpen on drums and Frank De La Rosa on bass.

Chapter 39
The 1971 Newport Jazz Festival
The Second Riot

The Southern rock group, The Allman Brothers Band, was scheduled to perform on opening night. Festival Field wasn't big enough to handle the large crowd.

The second night featured Dionne Warwick signing *What the World Needs Now is Love* when an unruly crowd of distraught youths, who had come a great distance and were denied tickets, crashed the fence.

The mob attacked the stage, destroyed some equipment and caused the immediate cancellation of the program.

Because of the riot, the festival would not return to Newport in 1972.

Producer George Wein was to transplant the festival to New York City, naming it the "Newport Jazz Festival-New York." George then expanded it to include performances at Yankee Stadium and Radio City Music Hall.

Chapter 40
The Festivals
In New York City, Boston and Saratoga

The 1972 Newport Jazz Festival-New York encompassed some 30 concerts, involving performances by 62 great talents. Included in this large group were Dizzy Gillespie, Duke Ellington, Dave Brubeck, Ray Charles and Roberta Flack.

In 1973, producer George Wein contracted Fenway Park in Boston, for a concert under the name "Newport-New England Jazz Festival."

They were all excellent performances. These programs continued through 1976 with significant musical success.

Burt Jagolinzer

In 1977, George moved the Newport Jazz Festival from New York City to the Saratoga Performing Arts Center. It was re-named again, the Newport Jazz Festival-Saratoga.

The financial support of corporate sponsors like Schlitz Beer and KOOL Cigarettes kept the festivals out of financial troubles.

Chapter 41
The New York City Years

Each year, the Newport Jazz Festival in New York featured dozens upon dozens of great performers.

My trips included regular quick stays as lodging and food in New York City can be very expensive. Also, I used the time to visit friends and sometimes relatives… and even sought out an occasional night spot visit to hear other jazz greats who happened to be performing in the area.

I caught the fabulous cabaret crooner Bobby Short at the Carlisle Hotel, pianist and vocalist Darryl Sherman at the Sheraton, brass specialist Ronnie Smithson, at the Old Pierre and saxophonist Illinois Jacquet at Basin Street West.

George Wein's New York performances were all over the city. Several also took place in Saratoga, a modest ride to the north. It was a challenge for me just to get there and return.

The talent at these shows was always top notch, mostly featuring his long-time friends in the business. Duke, Count, Brubeck and the great individual side men claimed most of the attention, yet new names began to surface, like the spectacular Wynton Marsalis on horn, his gifted brother Branford on reeds, Warren Vache and Nicholas Payton on trumpets, Michael Moore on bass (with his unusual humor), and Diana Krall at the ivories and vocals.

There were other New York events worth remembering, too, including a salute to clarinetist Benny Goodman, and a tribute to the great saxophonist, Charlie Parker. These performances were well attended and their work was truly outstanding.

George's New York stints were not to overshadow the other international festivals he produced all around the world. By this time George Wein had clearly become the leading jazz producer in the free-world. And jazz had been elevated to heights never before achieved.

George attempted to return to Newport, Rhode Island, in 1961 but it was not to be. This was a devastating void, not only for George, but to the overall economy in Newport as well. The festival week had become one of the most important financial weeks of the year in this small, special community. Many local businesses voiced their concern, but because of the riot that had taken place in the previous year, the festival had worn out its welcome and its license had been revoked.

The Newport City Council didn't allow George to return until 1981, after a ten year absence, and put many planning and operational reservations in place.

Yes, the festival was about to happen once again. Needless to say, I was delighted.

Chapter 42
The Special Voice of Johnny Hartman

During the late 70's, I had the good fortune to be attending a jazz night at Slade's Night Club owned by Basketball Hall of Famer, Bill Russell. It was located on Columbus Avenue in Boston, near Massachusetts Avenue.

It was my first and only visit there. It was also my only meeting with the late Johnny Hartman.

Johnny's unusual voice covered several ranges, from the deep bass to the beautiful baritone. He could sway you romantically into a ballad and slur his way into the deeper ending like no one that I had ever heard. Many women swooned over him.

At intermission that night, I was able to meet him, but only for a few quick moments. I asked, "Who has made the biggest impression on you?" Much to my surprise, he answered, "Bing Crosby and Caruso."

He passed away in 1983 at age 60.

To this day, I've never heard a voice even close to that of the late and great Johnny Hartman.

Chapter 43
The 1981 Newport Jazz Festival
The Return to Newport

After an unofficial sabbatical of ten years, the annual festival was back.

There was no question that the City of Newport had sorely missed the events for a long period of time. The economy had suffered dearly and local merchants lost a lot of money. Most business were eager to bring back this important musical week.

The jazz festival organization had paid their penalties and were hopeful for another chance. The producer, George Wein, wanted desperately to come back with a new proposal.

'Round Newport

The City agreed to allow the new program to take place at Fort Adams, an 1860 Army structure that was constructed by Irish builders brought to America by the U. S. Army just for this project. Many of the workers chose to remain in Newport after the project was completed. The fort was named after our second United States President, John Adams.

The Army had turned the fort over to the State of Rhode Island for recreational and cultural activities. The city was to make use of it for many important and unusual events.

The jazz festival had found a new home in Newport. It was to become a prime, seaside venue offering a free view of the concert to sailors and yachtsmen from spectacular Narragansett Bay. A daytime-only, alcohol-free format was approved.

And to everyone's delight, the "new" festival was immediately successful.

♫ ♫ ♫

Saturday

◆ Drummer **Mel Lewis's Orchestra**, featuring the talented reeds of Zoot Sims. The performance was outstanding.

◆ **Classic Jazz Band** led by the piano of Dick Hyman, the reeds of Bob Wilber, the upright bass of Major Holley, the drums of Oliver Jackson, the trombone of Vic Dickenson, with the trumpet of Doc Cheatham and the great Ruby Braff who performed on cornet. This combination was terrific.

◆ **Dexter Gordon** used his saxophone to work with the great Art Farmer on horn. Also playing with them were Major Holley, Oliver Jackson, Vic Dickenson and Doc Cheatham.

◆ **The McCoy Tyner Quintet** with McCoy at the piano. The great saxophonist John Coltrane was featured on several pieces.

◆ The fabulous **Buddy Rich Orchestra** was next, featuring Buddy's elongated solos on the drums. It was really cool.

♫ ♫ ♫

Sunday

◆ **Art Blakey and The Jazz Messengers** featured the reeds of Benny Golson and Johnny Griffin.

◆ **The Dave Brubeck Quartet** with Bill Smith followed on reeds. The group's great alto saxophonist, Paul Desmond, had passed away on May 30, 1977. This was their first appearance in Newport since losing him. The talented Bill Smith tried to fill Paul's shoes. Bill was great. The quartet were their usual

Bob Wilber

sensation particularly when their classic signature song, *Take Five*, brought everyone to their feet.

◆ **Nancy Wilson** performed next. She was certainly at the peak of her career and the audience loved her American Songbook numbers, as did I.

◆ **Dizzy Gillespie's Quartet** featured guest star Milt Jackson at his vibes. The music was outstanding. Dizzy then led a jam session that starred Al Grey on trombone, Buddy Tate on the reeds and the fabulous piano of Providence's Mike Renzi, among others.

◆ **Lionel Hampton** ended the festival that year with his full orchestra. Hamp was truly at his best and the event closed in style.

The festival was a success, a success vitally needed by both George Wein and the City of Newport.

Chapter 44
The 1982 Newport Jazz Festival

Saturday

◆ **The Rhode Island High School Jazz All-Star Ensemble** began. Their arrangements and choice of music accentuated the individual talents of the performers. They were terrific!

◆ **Mel Torme** followed with his usual magnificent voice. His honing of hand-picked favorites from Cole Porter, Johnny Mercer, Irving Berlin and George Gershwin delighted us all. We could never get enough of Mel.

◆ **Gerry Mulligan** and his orchestra took the stage and mesmerized the audience. And, of course, he was featured with his deep baritone saxophone. Their rhythm and sound created great music for us.

◆ **George Shearing** on piano and **Don Thompson** on bass performed next. They were listed as **The Duo**. It was a great performance with Shearing at his best. Their music was a perfect placement after the sound of Mulligan's big band orchestra.

◆ The **MJQ (Modern Jazz Quartet)** featuring John Lewis on the keys, Milt Jackson on vibes, Percy Heath at the bass and Connie Kay on drums blended beautifully.

◆ **Dorothy Donegan**, jazz pianist with Page Cavanaugh, singer and pianist were two west coast performers. Their gig was excellent.

◆ Trumpeter **Dick Sudhalter** played brilliantly, accompanied by the voice and piano of Rhode Island's own Daryl Sherman. They ended the Saturday afternoon show in style.

♪ ♪ ♪

Sunday

◆ The spectacular pianist **Oscar Peterson** was clearly at his best. He was accompanied by Herb Ellis on guitar and Ray Brown on the bass. They captured me and the audience. Oscar's flare for Cole Porter highlighted their performance.

◆ **The Sarah Vaughan Trio** performed next with Butch Lacy at the keys and Harold Jones on the drums. Sarah was at her finest. She bobbled and scatted through *Funny Valentine* and other hits to our delight. It was wonderful!

Chick Corea

◆ **The Great Quartet** was put together with Freddie Hubbard on the horn, McCoy Tyner at the keyboard, Ron Carter on the bass and Elvin Jones at the drums. It was a gas. They rocked the place.

◆ **Chick Corea and Gary Burton** followed with Chick on piano and Gary on vibes. They were complemented by four string players. Their sound was very new, and was even questioned by jazz critics at the time.

◆ It was time for **Red Norvo** on vibes and **Tal Farlow** on the guitar. They were accompanied by Steve Novasel on the bass. It was a fitting ending to a great weekend of wonderful jazz.

Chapter 45
The 1983 Newport Jazz Festival

Saturday

◆ **The Oscar Peterson Trio** opened the 1983 program. Oscar was on piano, Herb Ellis on guitar and Ray Brown on the bass. Oscar's rendition of two of Cole Porter's numbers highlighted their performance.

◆ **Stan Getz's** sound cannot be duplicated. He and his group were wonderful.

◆ **Spyro Gyra's** work was not jazz, but R&B. I wondered why they would even bring this group to the jazz festival. But after a while I began to appreciate their talent, that included the great reeds of Jay Beckenstein. And the audience did enjoy them.

Burt Jagolinzer

1983 Kool Jazz Festival Program

181

◆ **Carmen McRae** and her magnificent voice was next. Carmen, still at the peak of her long career, brought peace to the event with her delivery of selections from the Great American Songbook. My friends and I had been waiting for Carmen. We were not disappointed. It made our day.

◆ **Gato Barbieri** and his saxophone with the Oscar Peterson Trio behind him played next. His tone and boldness held the full attention of the audience. It was a fitting gig to end the Saturday afternoon event.

♬ ♬ ♬

Sunday

◆ The great **Ella Fitzgerald**, accompanied by Paul Smith at the piano began the day. The audience stood up for her and during most of her gig. Ella was at the top of her career and delighted us all. We were in heaven.

◆ **Dizzy Gillespie, Art Blakey and the Jazz Messengers**, featuring Terence Blanchard on horn followed Ella. They blew out the place with battle after battle of rich jazz sound. You knew that you were at a jazz festival for sure; this being jazz at its best.

◆ The trumpets of **Freddie Hubbard** and **Jon Faddis**, with the addition of young Wynton Marsalis on horn and his brother Branford on saxophone began performing. This continued the string of blow-out performances that day. It was dynamite.

◆ **George Wein's Festival All-Stars** ended the Sunday afternoon program and the weekend. George was at the piano with Providence's Scott Hamilton on tenor sax, Warren Vache on trumpet, Vic Dickenson on trombone, Slam Stewart on bass and Oliver Jackson on drums. Their improvisations were everywhere, yet their wonderful melodies were always recognizable. This set ranked among my favorite jazz presentations from a weekend of many great moments.

Chapter 46
For the Love of Willie Love

In the 1980s, the Red Parrot Restaurant in downtown Newport hired a local saxophone player, Willie Love, along with his quartet.

Willie had relocated to Rhode Island from Pennsylvania many years before. While in Pennsylvania, he had a regular gig which featured among his group an excellent guitar player.

According to Willie, his guitar player got sick one night, and someone recommended a kid by the name of George Benson as a replacement.

George continued playing with Willie's group, eventually deciding to go out on his own, attempting to make it big. Willie and George kept in touch.

George Benson was among the headliners one Friday evening at the Newport Jazz Festival. After his performance, he visited Willie and his quartet, at The Red Parrot Restaurant.

I was among the crowd welcoming George that night. He told the audience that his love for Willie, "reflected his name." He performed with Willie's group and it was very special.

That night, he hung around with Willie, just like old times. Those of us who attended will never forget this reunion of two talented men, who, because of music, kept their important personal connection alive.

Chapter 47
The 1984 Newport Jazz Festival

In 1984, Japanese Video Corporation (JVC) became the official major sponsor of the festival.

The talent committee had decided to favor the younger generation's music taste, beginning a move away from the normal commitment to the standard jazz performers.

◆ **Ray Charles** was at the top of the R&B charts when he opened the 1984 Newport program. Ray, who was on his piano, featured the Rayettes, a group of upbeat female dancers who danced and sang along with Ray, and his famous orchestra. It was a show by itself within a show. It was movin' and groovin'. The audience kept clapping and beating. Many of us thought we had received our money's worth already, and the show was just beginning.

JVC Newport Jazz Festival Sign

◆ **David Sanborn** with his wonderful saxophone and group had to follow this spectacle. Sanborn's sound was terrific and proved his quick rise to global popularity.

◆ **Dizzy Gillespie's Quartet** performed next with Dizzy on his famous bent-horn, and James Moody on reeds, Louis Bellson on drums and Ron Carter at the bass. They were loud and upbeat and the audience loved it.

◆ **Michel Petrucciani** surprised most of us. This little guy was absolutely spectacular at the piano. He presented tune after tune in an original style, and caught the audience's attention. He truly captured a piece of the jazz world during that excellent performance.

◆ **Tiger's Baku** was a fusion group led by trumpeter Tiger Okoshi, which followed next. Their music did not appeal to the tastes of my friends and me, but they certainly had a following in the crowd, and received polite applause.

♫ ♫ ♫

Sunday

◆ **Miles Davis** and his band. Miles was Miles. He mixed high notes with low ones and off clashes with perfect resolve. No one except Miles could do it and get away with it. He entertained.

◆ **B. B. King and his Orchestra**. Because of the style of his music, many of us thought he and his orchestra didn't belong in this jazz setting. But we made the best of it, and actually enjoyed his wild presentations and melodies.

◆ **Dave Brubeck** and his quartet had to follow this event. They settled the audience down with their classic, *Take Five*, and other favorites. Dave was at the piano, with Bill Smith on saxophone. Brubeck had started to bring his two talented sons into his gigs, Darius on the keyboards, and Danny on trombone and electric bass guitar. It was the beginning of a new era in the music of Dave Brubeck.

◆ Ronald Shannon Jackson was at the drums, leading a group called **The Decoding Society**. The group blasted away with funk and fusion, but was not to our liking. I found there was too much noise and the clashing of sounds were quite irregular. Although we have all now recognized that these are truly jazz performers, their music is more revered by the emerging market of newer jazz fans.

Chapter 48
Memorable Times with Dave McKenna

The late Dave McKenna, one of the greatest jazz pianists of the last century, had a regular gig at Boston's Copley Hotel in the middle of Copley Square facing Boylston Street.

His job required that he play several nights per week in the lounge closest to the street. It was dimly lit with large comfortable tables and chairs.

Most people had no idea of Dave's talent, or his life-long accomplishments, let alone that he was playing here for peanuts compared to the paycheck he earned when performing at some of the finest venues and events around the world.

This was truly a "fill-in" gig within reasonable distance to his apartment in Rhode Island and access to his son and family in nearby Cape Cod. He had been brought up in Rhode Island, becoming one of the favorite sons of the city of Woonsocket.

During the 1970's and part of the 80's, I would find time to cull the greater-Boston area for jazz of all kinds. I discovered Dave at the Copley Hotel.

I would catch him during the week as the weekends usually afforded him bigger and more profitable events elsewhere. Tuesdays, Wednesdays and Thursdays, though, he would be there for sure. Being an upscale hotel, people were generally well-dressed and there was a dress-code enforced for that lounge.

I would enter with shirt, jacket and tie and seek the best (closest) seat to his piano. Often it would be right next to his keyboard. How lucky I was.

Not being an alcohol imbiber, I would sip my way through the night with decaf-coffee. Amazingly, there was never a cover charge. And so, with a decent tip, I could spend several hours with this gifted performer almost for free.

Dave and I became good friends. Many nights I was the only one in the place clapping for him. In his own way, he appreciated my acknowledgement of his talent.

Dave played the numbers that had made him famous, and discussed the background of most of them privately with me. He shared the stories that went with each melody, pleased to have found someone truly interested in his own personal jazz experiences.

These became special times for me. I became privy to his best moments as a professional musician.

He performed without written music showing his skills and familiarity with many of the great sounds of the past, as well as the newer sounds in the mainstream. His improvisations were terrific and often highlighted his total presentation.

Like many musicians, performing for a whole evening, he would run out of regular numbers and would take on audience requests. I would often suggest a list of other titles that prompted his recollection.

Dave liked my lists and would play most of the compositions just for me.

Dave played for five presidents including Truman, Eisenhower, Kennedy, Nixon and Carter. Dave was especially proud of those moments. He had recorded with some three to four hundred different musical groups during his days and had traveled most of the world performing for kings, queens and potentates.

Burt Jagolinzer

When he passed away in 2008, I reflected on the special and enlightening times I enjoyed with this immensely talented giant of jazz.

Chapter 49
The 1985 Newport Jazz Festival

Saturday

◆ **The Dirty Dozen Brass Band** opened the 1985 festival with a bang. Kirk Joseph on the tuba highlighted the Dixieland presentation. It got the whole event going in the right direction. It was cool, to say the least.

◆ Performing next was trumpet great **Freddie Hubbard**, with Cedar Walton at the piano, Richie Cole on the alto, Billy Hart at the drums and Buster Williams on bass. They were loud and blended together wonderfully.

◆ "Sassy" **Sarah Vaughan** was to follow. She was accompanied by George Gaffney at the piano, Andy Simpkins on bass and Harold Jones on the drums. Sarah was certainly still at the peak of her career. She performed number after number featuring ballads by Jerome Kern, Hoagy Carmichael and John Mercer. It was heaven for my friends and me.

◆ The slate ended with **Spyro Gyra** blasting away. Jay Beckenstein on reeds was featured. Their fans were ready, and they went wild, just as they had done back in 1983 at their previous performance at Newport. Although it was not exactly jazz in my opinion, my friends and I did enjoy the band's enthusiasm and upbeat rhythms.

♫ ♫ ♫

Sunday

◆ Opening next day was **The David Murray Octet** with David and his reeds as the feature performer. It was groovy.

◆ **The McCoy Tyner Quartet** came next. Complementing McCoy on piano were Arthur Blythe on saxophone, Louis Hayes on drums and Avery Sharpe on the bass. Their music and sound were terrific.

◆ **Lee Ritenour** and **Dave Grusin**. Lee with his trusty guitar and Dave on the keyboards truly entertained us all.

◆ It was time for **The Wynton Marsalis Quartet** with Wynton on horn, Marcus Roberts on piano, Charnett Moffett at the bass and Jeff Watts on the drums. Wynton's formal presentation and perfections were evident throughout their performance. Marcus Roberts was sensational on the piano, as was Wynton with his trumpet solos. To many of my friends, it was the best moment of the evening.

The Return of Miles Davis

◆ But the younger crowd had come to see and hear **Stevie Ray Vaughan and Double Trouble** that day. Stevie had become an eclectic fiery guitarist and had an impressive singing range. He and his group had ignited the country revival of rock and roll blues. Their fans went crazy. The jazz audience couldn't believe what was happening. The place went absolutely nuts.

Stevie was accompanied by Reese Wynans on the piano, Jack Newhouse at the bass and Chris Layton on drums.

Stevie Vaughan was to die tragically in a helicopter crash in 1990 at the age of just thirty six.

It was a memorable and unusual way to end this Sunday program and the annual festival.

Chapter 50
Sudhalter and Sherman

Sudhalter and Sherman spent two summers in Rhode Island, before returning to their established base in New York City.

It was 1984 when Daryl Sherman, one of the prides of Woonsocket, opted to bring her talented voice and piano skills back to the Ocean State. With her came Dick Sudhalter, a Bostonian who had become quite famous as an excellent trumpet player, jazz critic and author, among many other attributes.

They worked several gigs together, including Newport's Treadway Hotel and Narragansett's Coast Guard House.

I followed them, enjoying their unique renditions from the Great American Songbook. They were entertaining and a lot of fun to watch.

Burt Jagolinzer

Unfortunately, Dick passed away in 2008 at the age of sixty nine. Daryl continues her profession today in New York City, with performances at a variety of hotels and clubs, and occasional gigs in Europe and elsewhere.

Chapter 51
The 1986 Newport Jazz Festival

Saturday

◆ **The Rhode Island Youth Band** began the day. Their arrangements and music were as highly professional as any performing orchestra that had performed here in the past. Their solos were outstanding, featuring some of the jazz world's future players. They were a credit to musical educators here in the Ocean State.

◆ **The John Scofield Group** was next. Their music bordered on funk, with strong R&B roots. My friends and I debated whether we thought their music belonged at this event. Either way, John's guitar and original music stood out.

◆ **The Gerry Mulligan Quartet** followed. Mulligan was certainly at the peak of his career. Among the standards, he

Burt Jagolinzer

Gerry Mulligan

mixed in several of his own compositions that were well received by the audience.

Gerry Mulligan's deep baritone saxophone had become easily recognizable throughout the jazz world.

◆ **Michael Franks** and a group of accompanists took over the stage next. Michael, a west coast product, caught us by surprise. With a guitar in his hands, he sang wonderful light compositions that ignited the fans. His own hit song, *Popsicle Toes*, brought cheers from the audience. His performance was one of the highlights of the day.

◆ **Stanley Jordan** performed next. A truly gifted guitarist from Chicago, with a strong background in music from Princeton University, he performed mostly in a rock-type style. His music touched traditional jazz but kept moving away during the performance.

◆ **Miles Davis** and his band took over the stage. Miles began playing with his back to the audience. We weren't sure why. Had he lost his confidence? Whatever the reason, it was Miles. And Miles was Miles. His music was becoming "way-out," but the fans still loved it, and, for the most part, we did too. It was not the usual way to end the concert, yet, we went away truly remembering another special Miles Davis performance.

♫ ♫ ♫

Sunday

◆ Soprano saxophone guru **Wayne Shorter** began the day. By this time in his career, he had switched from tenor to soprano, and his funky presentation was an encouragement for younger players hopeful to make it in the fusion-jazz world. He and his group made a lot of noise with their clash of offbeat music, creating an abundance of sharps and flats new to the Newport scene. I thought it was just too much.

◆ **George Howard,** the well-known composer and soprano saxophonist followed. He and his group had moved toward a funk style in their opening numbers. From there, it was hard to appreciate his music or his melodies. Yet, the audience clapped throughout the gig.

◆ **Miss Natalie Cole** was to hit on all cylinders. Her voice was terrific, proving that she was one of the top female singers in the world. We all reflected on how proud her late father would have been had he been alive to see and hear her performance. Her personal renditions from the American Song Book were outstanding and she slayed us with her chosen ballads. Many of us had come just to hear her alone. She captured the day's events.

◆ **Al DiMeola**, composer and noted jazz funk guitarist came next. He and his group performed in fusion-funk styles with an interesting Latin-American influence evident in most of his numbers.

◆ The great **David Sanborn** was to follow. The quality of David's tone was the real feature. His rise in popularity was based on that special saxophone sound, and we got plenty of it during this ending set.

Chapter 52
A Musician's Life in New York City

During the 1986 Newport festival at Fort Adams State Park, I met the kid brother of great tenor saxophonist David Sanborn outside the performers' fence. He was nearly a clone of David.

I learned we were both waiting for David to come out. I was hoping to talk to him He was scheduled to perform with a small group and end the Sunday portion and the event.

Natalie Cole and her quintet had wooed the audience just before his gig.

David's career was peaking. He was living in New York, playing with excellent groups all around the city. He had even played with the David Letterman Orchestra and had been syndicated on a national radio show. He was considered to be one of the finest reedmen in this country at the time.

Yet his brother told me that David was washing dishes several evenings per week, earning extra money, in order to afford to stay in New York City.

I couldn't believe it. When David finally came to greet us he quickly admitted to the employ. He soon changed the subject to music and the just completed festival.

That day, my friends and I learned about the limited income that many of the top jazz talent were living on. We believe it must change. Professional jazz artists, like David Sanborn, need to receive higher wages for their efforts.

No doubt we the patrons will be asked to pay more to help make that happen.

Chapter 53
The 1987 Newport Jazz Festival

Saturday

◆ **Nancy Wilson.** Miss "Elegance" swooned us with several ballads from the American Songbook. Her singing style and grace stood alone during this important part of her career. We loved it.

◆ **Wynton Marsalis** was just twenty five years-old and had an unprecedented two Grammy Awards to his credit for both jazz and classical recordings. He dazzled the audience with his skills and perfection on trumpet. There was evidence that he had become the master of the horn with jazz excellence. My friends and I believe that few trumpet players can come close to his delivery or his demeanor.

◆ Extraordinary guitarist **Stanley Jordan** was next. He and his group mesmerized the crowd with previously unheard tunes and original presentation. His unique skills on the guitar quickly captured our attention. His gig was exceptional.

◆ Saxophonist **Kenny G.** was to perform next. He ran the limits for his instrument, touching waves of jazz into the modern sounds that have attracted the younger crowd. And, his good looks got the female audience to scream and holler, too. His presentation was different.

◆ Joe Sample on the keyboard, with Wilton Felder on sax and bass, led the **Crusaders** band. Their Texas background blended with sounds that crossed between jazz and rock. Their loyal fans loved the performance, but it was not to my taste.

♫ ♫ ♫

Sunday

◆ **George Benson** came across the stage. Already at the top of his popularity, George swooned the ballads with his gifted voice. His guitar skills came next and we loved it. George is a winner, appreciated by most of the audience. It was a great choice for the day's opener.

◆ **Branford Marsalis** (brother of Wynton) followed with his reeds. He blended beautifully with his group, taking on an occasional solo.

◆ **Dianne Reeves'** voice then resonated throughout the park. She sang mostly African chants, focusing on the rhythm rather than the melodies. Her beauty and confident presentation highlighted her performance.

◆ **The Michael Brecker Band** performed next. Michael's tenor saxophone reached out to a new version of jazz-rock. His group blasted away with original compositions. It was not my kind of music, but he did have a following, and a sizable group applauded after each number.

◆ **Dizzy Gillespie** fronted his big band to close-out the day. They performed popular orchestrations and some "way-out" fusion type compositions. The mix worked well with most of the audience. We clapped and danced to their loud and fiery arrangements. It was an interesting way to end the weekend festival.

Chapter 54
The 1988 Newport Jazz Festival

Saturday

◆ The day began with a tribute to the great **Lionel Hampton**, featuring his big orchestra. They were outstanding in rhythm and sound.

◆ **Grover Washington, Jr.** Grover's clarinet solos were special with masterful slurs that would separate him from other clarinet performers. His performance was wonderful.

◆ Boston's own **Chick Corea** was to follow. His keyboard gig was known to be in a jazz-fusion style. And though his young fans were in heaven, we found his music difficult to appreciate.

◆ From Rochester, New York, came the talented flugel-horn player **Chuck Mangione**. His sweet tone caressed his performance of many hand-picked ballads from another era. New compositions were performed with his instrument in high gear. We enjoyed his different approach to some of the old standards.

◆ **Montgomery, Plant and Stritch** were next. They were a trio of two gals and a guy whose voices did a great job on several old pop standards, jazz numbers and a few sophisticated show tunes, without accompaniment. Critics applauded. We, too, thought their performance was terrific.

◆ **The Rhode Island Youth Stage Band** was to finish the day. Their talent was sensational and it proved an excellent ending to a full day of music.

♫ ♫ ♫

Sunday

◆ Keyboardist **Herbie Hancock** and his trio began the event. Performing along with Herbie was drummer Al Foster and bassist Buster Williams. Some of their music was difficult to understand, but the rest was quite good. The audience received them with vigor.

◆ **The Carmen McRae Quartet** followed. Carmen, still at the peak of her long career, was spectacular. Her gifted voice hung on the emotional lyrics of the wonderful composers. Among the group supporting her was the saxophone guru, Dexter Gordon, also at his best. This was a special gig and I knew it.

◆ **B. B. King** and his famous guitar he called "Lucille" took center stage. Together, with his accompanists, he entertained us all. His performance exemplified the importance of the blues in the jazz art form. Everyone loved his presentation.

◆ **The Count Basie Orchestra** performed next. "The Count" Bill Basie, who had started his musical career as a silent-movie pianist at the Elbon Theatre in the 1930's in Kansas City, passed away in the fall of 1984. But his band and their famous music were picked-up by his long-time trusted saxophone player, Frank Foster. Frank was to front the orchestra for several more years.

Frank kept the sound together with Basie's orchestrations and swing tradition. He made it seem as if The Count was still with us. The music was unforgettable.

◆ **Najee**, the New York born saxophonist was the final performer. He was a graduate of the New England Conservatory of Music. His performance featured original compositions and sounds that were derived from the bebop style. It was a disappointing choice to end the festival.

Chapter 55
The 1989 Newport Jazz Festival

Saturday

◆ **The Rhode Island Youth Stage Band**, under the direction of Ted Collins began at 11 a.m. Their music featured excellent arrangements and was professionally performed by the many talented school musicians who had been chosen from around the state. They were awesome.

◆ **Wynton Marsalis** and his trumpet followed. Returning to the Newport stage, he brought outstanding hand-picked musicians and the group performed to perfection. Their musical selections were also pre-determined by Wynton himself. He led this imposing group with his own trumpet solos.

◆ Then the voice of **Dianne Reeves** rang throughout the park. Her rhythm and focus had a true African musical influence, and her loud voice caught the audience. Many stood and danced to her chosen rhythm. It was catchy.

◆ **Branford Marsalis** was next. As expected, Branford hit on all cylinders and his music was special. Everyone enjoyed his group's recital.

◆ Saxophonist **Herbie Mann** had decided to switch to flute. He became one of the first reedmen to do so. While in South America he picked up on their special rhythm and beat. Soon, he was touted as one of the top flutists in the world. His sounds were quite different and attractive. His established fans and new ones appreciated his new delivery on stage.

◆ **Spyro Gyra** was to complete the day. Once again, Jay Beckenstein stole the performance. His saxophone highlighted their presentation, and as you might guess, their fans were rock-in'.

♫ ♫ ♫

Sunday

◆ The fabulous **Jimmy Smith Trio** began the event. Complementing Jimmy at the organ were Houston Person on saxophone and Jon Faddis on trumpet. Person had been around for a while, while Faddis was relatively new to the jazz scene. Jon Faddis blew us away. His range caught everyone by surprise. The performance convinced us that he would have to be included among the great horn players available in this part of the country.

◆ **Tuck and Patti** took stage next. Tuck Andress and Patti Cathcart met at an audition in 1978, married, and became singing R&B legends in the western part of the country. This was their first appearance in Newport. Many fans had followed them here and appreciated their performance. It was certainly professional, but the sounds were not for me.

◆ **The Dave Brubeck Quartet** was next. As usual, they performed renditions of the many hits that made them famous. And as expected, *Take Five* exploded from their instruments and the audience went crazy. I was affected as well.

◆ **The Dizzy Gillespie Quartet** was next. Dizzy and his bent horn came across the stage next and people cheered. They unloaded with rhythm and clash and dancing in the aisles quickly became the norm. I got up and joined in. He and his group were in high gear.

◆ **David Sanborn** had the unenviable task of following Dizzy, and he gave us his very best on his trusty saxophone. To his credit, the fans stayed around to appreciate and applaud his terrific effort.

Chapter 56
Dissecting a Few of the Greats

Dizzy Gillespie was an important gift to jazz. Like many of the successful musicians of his day, he had within him the need to succeed with his instrument, via his own presentation, and the desire to leave a legacy that few would ever match.

He was an extrovert, witty, and fiery. His horn had to be different, and it was. He was an innovator, with imagination and inventiveness.

Dizz was a major part of the "new thing" in jazz. Working with saxophonist Charlie Parker, Thelonious Monk on the keys, and Milt Hinton on the bass, they experimented and found entirely new directions.

Because of their already high regard in the industry, the new music was immediately accepted. But, only select individuals truly took to it.

Dizzy could get wild at times, and in his later years, he put on several controversial shows. His connection to African music became a highlight of his performances.

His special sound and bent-horn will never be forgotten.

Miles Davis had, in his early days, become a master trumpeter to his generation. Sadly drugs took over, and down he went. He seemed to be continually plagued with personal trauma and artistic inactivity.

Miles returned surprisingly in 1955, when George Wein gave him the chance to perform at Newport. Even though his name was not on the program that year, he was to blow the place apart. His new sound and approach was reported to be entirely different, and it was.

He released some recordings and his popularity rose once again.

Chapter 57
My Trumpet on a CD

Long after I retired from serious playing, my trusty cornet laid dormant in its original case for years.

For a unique Father's Day present, my son Andy had me meet up with him at a friend's house. "Don't ask any questions," he pleaded, "but bring along your trumpet."

Andy had become a rock and roll music guru. As a youngster, he loved this diverse music style and was a walking encyclopedia on rock, its performers and its changing methods and language. He had served as a lead-singer in a small group that attempted to make it to the big time. They called themselves Delta Clutch. Unfortunately, after several years of performing and traveling, they never found the break needed to make it commercially. Andy eventually broke away, choosing to go in a different direction.

To my surprise, the friend's house he had me visit was also a studio, full of the state-of-the-art electronics of the day. He placed me downstairs in an open room with just a microphone hanging from the ceiling. On the stool under the mic was a set of headphones. He instructed me to put the headphones on.

Following his musical direction, I played some interesting chords and riffs and the mic picked-up my diverse horn sounds. This session went on for nearly an hour.

Then I was asked to close up my instrument and come upstairs to the main studio. Here, I was treated to several recordings of my son's group's latest original compositions that had been skillfully mixed in that studio.

Finally, they played a number that they had dubbed with my trumpet -- the riffs and sounds were brought into the composition brilliantly. I was truly taken by what had happened.

At the end of this session, Andy presented me with a copy of my own CD which was their latest with me in it. I was so proud and excited.

Many of my friends and family listened patiently to this CD. I will never forget that special moment and this unique present.

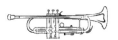

Chapter 58
The 1990 Newport Jazz Festival

◆ **The Count Basie Orchestra,** now under the direction of their great saxophone player Frank Foster began. The music, as usual, was sensational. The arrangements included many solos that delighted us all.

◆ **The Elvin Jones Jazz Machine** was next on the schedule. Elvin was a wiz on drums, and his brother Hank sat at the piano to lead the group. Others in the group included the saxophones of Sonny Fortune and Ravi Coltrane, John's son. The music was heavy and loud, and the crowd applauded throughout.

◆ **Joe Zawinul's Syndicate** came next. Joe, an Austrian-American jazz keyboardist and composer, had co-developed fusion-jazz with Miles Davis. He was accompanied by Bill Summers on percussion, Randy Bernsen on guitar, Gerald Veasley on the bass and Bobby Thomas, Jr. on the hand-drums. They made a lot of noise, but their rhythm was awesome and their fans kept movin' and groovin'.

Frank Weiss of the Count Basie Orchestra

◆ **Tito Puente** and the music changed to a Latin groove. Tito Puente and his large orchestra caught the audience by surprise, and his music was contagious. We were dancing in the aisles again.

◆ **Celia Cruz** was to end the day. Her beautiful voice followed and blessed the crowd with plenty of upbeat, loud Spanish sounds.

Chapter 59
The 1991 Newport Jazz Festival

◆ **Lou Rawls'** performance at the 1991 festival was his first at Newport. His unique, deep, smooth voice made many new fans that day. They swooned over the romantic delivery of his ballads. Although I had listened to him on the radio for several years, watching him perform only increased my appreciation for his talent.

◆ **The Jazz Futures** were to follow. Led by trumpeter Roy Hargrove, he was accompanied by Mark Whitfield at the guitar, Antonio Hart on alto sax, Tim Warfield on the tenor, Marlon Jordan on horn, Christian McBride on the bass, Carl Allen on the drums and Benny Green on piano. Their sounds and rhythm blew the place away. They played hard and loud and the audience and I loved it.

◆ **John Lee Hooker**, the American blues singer and composer, followed with an acoustic blues set not heard before at Newport. His music was more country-western, and not necessarily jazz. The fans enjoyed it anyway, and they showed their appreciation with constant applause.

◆ **The "Queen of Soul" Miss Etta James** followed. The six time Grammy Award-winner blended religious music with soul, blues and jazz. She had been known as "Miss Peaches," and the loveliness of her complexion served the name well. She captivated her many loyal fans and created some new ones.

◆ Dominican Republic's spectacular pianist **Michel Camilo** came on stage and held our attention throughout his entire performance. The chords he played on both his left and right hands seemed new and aggressive. He was awesome, to say the least.

Chapter 60
Jazz in Europe

My former-spouse Marsha joined the local Sweet Adeline's Chorus, a ladies equivalent to a men's barbershop, and put her talented voice to work.

Attracted by the four-part harmony, I decided to join the men's group. Prior to that, I had some experienced from a singing trip I took to Europe with a classical orchestra from New York State.

These singing excursions piqued my interest in this music field. I accepted the challenge of bringing musical groups from America to Europe, and visa-versa.

For the next ten years, I was to do it as a personal hobby and for the love of the art form. It was not a money-maker nor was it designed to do so. It was a terrific and enjoyable challenge that helped me make wonderful friendships. I relished being part of so many successful musical journeys. It was a unique experience both for me and for the many people I worked with.

I became a regular traveler to Europe, developing structured programs for these musical groups and their performances. I became familiar and enjoyed the many cities and destinations that make up a good amount of European culture.

I searched these cities for jazz, and was fortunate to attend many exceptional events and performances during this period.

On a recent trip to Italy, I even had the chance to sing at the front entrance to La Scala, considered to be the Mecca for opera singing, located in Milan.

Chapter 61
The 1992 Newport Jazz Festival

◆ The exciting voice of **Roberta Flack** was the leading feature of the 1992 Newport Jazz Festival. Her sound touched on both soul and R&B. It was quite evident that she had many fans attending as they cheered, clapped and never seemed to stop. Roberta worked hard to give them what they came to see and hear.

◆ Also that year was **The New York Jazz Giants** led by Tom Harrell on the flugelhorn, with Jon Faddis on trumpet, Lew Tabackin on tenor, Bobby Watson on alto, Ray Drummond at the bass and Carl Allen on drums. They were sensational. What a team! They kept the audience dazzled throughout their show. It was totally upbeat.

◆ **T. S. Monk**, son of Thelonious Monk, took stage with his group. T.S. had developed into a veteran jazz drummer on his own, and his accompanists followed him. They produced very credible and entertaining music in their first Newport performance.

◆ **The Max Roach Quartet** was next. Max was a brilliant drummer and vocalist. He was accompanied by Idrees Sulieman on horn, Leon Comegys on trombone, and Walter Davis at the piano. Their music was both bebop and hard bop. They made a lot of noise and had fans cheering.

◆ James Brown's backing band, now called **J. B. Horns**, took over the stage. Their music featured a funk style, with ongoing rhythm. Clashes of melodies came within their performance. It was not my kind of music. They featured Maceo Parker and Pee Wee Ellis on saxophones, with Fred Wesley on trombone.

◆ **The Tower of Power** had attracted a large following. This California group gave a funky soul sound featuring an R&B based horn section. Emilio Castillo led the band on saxophone, while Stephen Kupka blended with his baritone sax. They, too, made a lot of noise, but it was not my kind of jazz music.

Chapter 62
Classical Jazz, At its Best

Back in the late 1980's, while visiting my family in Arizona, my brother Ken, his wife Ruthie, and I attended a concert at the Scottsdale Civic Auditorium that featured the three finest classical guitar players in the world, at that time.

We were privy to the sensational work of Charlie Byrd, Herb Ellis and Barney Kessel. They were performing without accompaniment. In this format, each had their own chance to show their best.

Then when they performed together, their strumming chords and melodies shook my inner frame.

They were on a limited tour. We all agreed that we had been attending an historic performance. The group continued performing until unfortunately, a short time later, Barney Kessel died and broke up the team.

We will never forget the live performance and how lucky we were to have had the chance to hear these three masters at the peak of their sensational careers.

Chapter 63
The 1993 Newport Jazz Festival

◆ The **Ray Charles** organization was featured on the 1993 Newport program. As usual, Ray brought along his entire entourage. Ray's piano playing was still the attraction, as was expected, and his soul numbers were performed to perfection. The Rayettes, his back-up group formerly known as The Cookies, included a group of singers and dancers that graced the performance. Their fans clapped and danced. Though bluesy, the tone was upbeat throughout. It was a remarkable presentation. We had to remember that the blues and soul continue to be a great and important part of jazz. Many of us thought we received our money's worth just from this historic performance alone.

◆ Young **Joshua Redman** followed with his tenor saxophone. Redman had just graduated from Harvard University. He had been accepted at Yale University Law School, but opted to put it off for a year. Having achieved success in jazz, I don't believe he has yet to attempted an education in law. His talent was recognizable from the start. It was his first Newport experience, but you wouldn't have known it. He and his group were terrific.

◆ Dominican Republic's **Michel Camilo** returned to the Newport stage. His 1991 gig was not easily forgotten, and his performance on this day was again spectacular. Newfound fans applauded right along with the old. His different piano interpretation was well received. His talent remains very special.

◆ **The Brecker Brothers**, Michael on saxophone with Randy on trumpet, made up the entirety of this group. The music was loud and upbeat and most of us enjoyed their presentation. They received generous applause and they deserved it.

Chapter 64
The 1994 Newport Jazz Festival

Saturday

◆ **The Manhattan Transfer** began performing. Their modern voice arrangements fractured the audience with their original interpretations of the American Songbook. I felt they were at their peak of success and deserved their huge following. The music was sensational. I loved their performance.

◆ **Wynton Marsalis** was to return to Newport. Wynton's trumpet sounds were that of perfection. As always, his work separated him from all other contemporary players.

◆ Next was **The Yellow Jackets**, a jazz fusion band, with R&B-like sounds. Featured was Bob Mintzer on the tenor and bass clarinet. Also featured was Mike Stern on guitar. The music was tough to understand, but the audience seemed to like it.

'Round Newport

◆ **Joe Lavano** took to the stage. Bop jazz veteran Joe Lovano teased us with his saxophone. He led his group brilliantly featuring some of his own compositions as well as a few old ones. Jazz lovers can really never get enough of Joe Lovano.

◆ Jazz stride pianist **Marcus Roberts** was next. Along with his accompanists, he tinkled the ivories with both modern jazz tunes and some original creations. The audience applauded at each tune's ending. It wasn't his first appearance. He had played here before with Wynton Marsalis.

◆ Songstress **Cassandra Wilson** was to end the event. She sang a series of country, blues and folk music, including one of her own original compositions. The day closed on a great note and we made our way home humming several of the songs from her performance.

♫ ♫ ♫

Sunday

◆ **David Sanborn** began the day. As in his several prior Newport gigs, he dazzled us with his saxophone. Now a veteran performer, he mixed several upbeat numbers in with his ballads. We all loved his work.

◆ R&B vocalist and guitar player, **Buddy Guy** sounded more country-western than R&B. He created a lot of noise and his fans were true to him throughout, but the sound was not consistent with contemporary jazz.

◆ **The Dirty Dozen Brass Band**'s music was strictly funk and bebop. Greg Davis led on vocal and horn, with Roger Lewis on the baritone sax, Kevin Harris on tenor, Terrence Higgins on the drums and Kirk Joseph on the sousaphone. The beat was rhythm at its peak. This performance lacked melody and again just didn't fit. Contemporary jazz singer, Rachelle Ferrell, followed. Many of her numbers were mainstream R&B, pop and Gospel. It was not my kind of music.

◆ **Terence Blanchard** took the stage. Composer, bandleader, arranger, American jazz trumpeter Terence Blanchard and jazz songstress Jeanie Bryson (daughter of Dizzy Gillespie) were to close out the day and the weekend. Their renditions of the Billie Holiday Songbook covered many of her famous tunes. Blanchard's horn and Jeanie's voice captivated us. It was a wonderful ending to this year's Newport program.

Chapter 65
The 1995 Newport Jazz Festival

◆ **Tito Puente and his Latin Jazz Ensemble** began the program. They were so upbeat that just about everybody was clapping or dancing -- the place went wild. The Latin numbers were delivered with such a defined sound and rhythm that many of us thought the rest of today's show might as well be finished. It was awesome.

◆ **Earl Klugh** followed. He was an American smooth jazz crossover-to-fusion guitarist and composer. His work included a potpourri of sweet original contemporary music. He entertained the audience but didn't hold my attention. The music was just not my style.

Burt Jagolinzer and George Wein at a Friday night cocktail party.

◆ **Rite of Strings** performed. It was total acoustical, featuring Jean-Luc Ponty on violin, Al Di Meola on guitar and Stanley Clarke on bass. They made plenty of noise and the fans reacted to their flare. Even though the music was melodic, I just couldn't bring myself to enjoy it.

◆ **Dr. Dorothy Donegan** was next. She was an American trained classical jazz pianist who played stride piano, boogie-woogie style and classical jazz as well. Her performance was quite different, featuring plenty of melody and wonderful chords.

◆ **Dianne Reeves** returned to Newport. Her performance this day resembled her prior Newport singing efforts. Once again, it was mostly African-style music, with plenty of fans and friends present.

◆ Ending the weekend event were **The Newport All-Stars**, featuring Warren Vache on horn, Urbie Green on trombone, Bill Easley on reeds, Mike LeDonne at the piano with Peter Washington on double-bass and brother Kenny Washington at the drums.

Chapter 66
The 1996 Newport Jazz Festival

Saturday

◆ **The Manhattan Transfer** opened the concert. It was to be their second performance at Newport and the crowd loved it. They hit on many ballads and standards taken from the American Songbook, taking the rhythm and sound to a new height. It was truly a great way to begin this Saturday afternoon show.

◆ **Chick Corea** was next, featuring Chick on piano. His music is always questionable in my mind, mixing original arrangements of varied composers, thereby creating strange sounds. Chick has always had his loyal fans and they loved his gig, but, I must admit that I get lost in his music. His dedication for this performance was in memory of reedman Bud Powell.

◆ Within the same memorial came **Joshua Redman** on tenor, Wallace Roney on horn, Christian McBride on bass and Roy Haynes on the drums. It was a smashing group with plenty of loud noise that really brought the audience to its feet.

◆ Next was **The McCoy Tyner Trio**, with special guest Michael Brecker with his reeds. McCoy was at his piano and at the top of his career. They played an upbeat tempo throughout, and it was great.

◆ **James Carter** took the stage. His tenor were featured in each number. His sound was dynamic and everyone seemed to enjoy the gig. Javon Jackson on tenor saxophone blended in and the rhythm continued.

◆ **Bruce Hornsby** was to end the day. The famous guitarist and composer captivated the audience, delivering original pieces as well as a few old ones.

♪ ♪ ♪

Sunday

◆ Singer-dancer **Al Jarreau** began. His musical numbers, though standards, were sung in a way that only Al Jarreau could perform. It is always different when you see and listen to this entertainer, and he brought along his faithful fan base to clap and applaud.

◆ **Ahmad Jamal** took over the stage. His smooth and original tinkling of the ivories separates him from other successful pianists of the day. His approach to the American standards is entirely different. His left-handed chords sparkle at the right moments, accentuating the composers' key areas.

◆ **Herbie Hancock** was next. Michael Brecker, with his saxophone, was his special guest. They wove their way around a long list of Herbie's hit tunes. His rendition of *Watermelon Man* brought down the house.

◆ **Spyro Gyra** and group took to the stage. As before, Jay Beckenstein on his reeds was featured. Their fans had come once again to hail their presentation. Their upbeat music caught everyone's attention.

◆ Italian guitarist **Pat Martino** was last to perform. Accompanying him in the quartet were Scott Robinson on saxophone, Steve Beskrone at the bass and James Ridl at the piano. They were awesome and a great way to end the day.

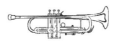

Chapter 67
Jazz Week in Newport

Back in 1996, our non-profit Newport Jazz Association decided to create "Newport Jazz Week." It was designed to supplement the Newport Jazz Festival produced by Festival Productions. Vice President, R. J. Von See, and I partnered to promote this idea. Our secretary, M. J. Harris, and treasurer Beverly Adler, played important roles as well.

We thought the event might serve to highlight the end of the week festival that would follow our activities. We hoped to get the local residents more excited about the weekend event. We also envisioned additional gigs for many of our local musicians.

We also hoped to get local Newport area businesses to sponsor the many events that we were planning.

Burt Jagolinzer

Newport Jazz Week

SPONSORED by the Newport Jazz Association, a non-profit organization with the motto, "keeping jazz alive and helping kids," this event takes place in Newport, unless noted on Aug. 5-12. Admission prices varies per event. Discounts with buttons purchased at local stores (346-0302) for $5. Call 847-3291 and 685-3575. See additional "Newport Jazz Week" events in the next issue of Newport This Week.

Sunday 5

Jazz Breakfast
Hotel Viking patio, 1 Bellevue Ave., 9am-1pm.

Opening Night Ceremony
Quaker Meeting Hall, 21 Farewell St., 847-3291, 7pm. Service in remembrance of deceased jazz greats. Ribbon cutting, special guests, US Navy Brass Group and Gospel choir.

Monday 6

Jazz Breakfast
Hotel Viking patio, 1 Bellevue Ave., 847-3291, 9am-1pm. Live jazz trio.

Jam Sessions
King Park bandstand, Wellington Ave., noon-6pm. Invited juried musicians.

Seniors' Jazz Tea & Swing Dance
Portsmouth Senior Center, 110 Bristol Ferry Road, Portsmouth, 683-4106, 1-4pm.

Jazz Brunch & Lunch
OceanCliff Hotel, 65 Ridge Road. Features Billy Weston.

Jazz at the Pier
Vincent's On the Pier, 10 Howard's Wharf. Features the Charlie Harris Group.

Jazz & Gospel
United Baptist Church, 30 Spring St., 847-3291, 7pm.

Jazz Ferry
RIPTA Newport/Providence ferry location, Perotti Park, America's Cup Ave.

Tuesday 7

Jazz Breakfast
Hotel Viking patio, 1 Bellevue Ave., 9am-1pm.

Jazz Sail
Aboard "Aurora," Goat Island, 10am, free with button.

Jam Sessions
King Park bandstand, Wellington Ave., 847-3291, noon-6pm. Invited juried musicians.

Jazz Lunch
Marina Pub, Goat Island.

Seniors' Jazz Tea & Swing Dance
Aquidneck Place Assisted Living, Off 138, Portsmouth, 1-4pm. Professional DJ.

Jazz Bar-B-Que
Jonathan's Restaurant, 167 Park Ave., Island Park, Portsmouth, 6pm. The Bermuda Strollers & the Gumby Dancers.

Jazz at the Beach
Easton's Beach, Memorial Blvd., 7pm. Dick Lupino & group.

Jazz Ferry
RIPTA Newport/Providence ferry location, Perotti Park, America's Cup Ave.

Wednesday 8

Jazz Breakfast
Hotel Viking patio, 1 Bellevue Ave., 9am-1pm. Live jazz trio.

Seminar
Edward King Senior Center, Aquidneck Park, 11am-noon. "How to Enjoy Jazz."

Jam Sessions
King Park bandstand, Wellington Ave., noon-6pm. Invited juried musicians.

Seniors' Jazz Tea & Swing Dance
Edward King Senior Center, Aquidneck Park, 846-7426, 1-2pm. Professional DJ.

Jazz Picnic & Concert
Newport Art Museum, 76 Bellevue Ave., 846-8200, 6pm.

Jazz with the Mayor
Sardella's Italian Restaurant, 30 Memorial Blvd., 8pm. Matt Quinn & others.

Jazz Ferry
RIPTA Newport/Providence ferry location, Perotti Park, America's Cup Ave.

Thursday 9

Jazz Breakfast
Hotel Viking patio, 1 Bellevue Ave., 9am-1pm. Live jazz trio.

Jam Sessions
King Park bandstand, Wellington Ave., noon-6pm. Invited juried musicians.

Seniors' Jazz Tea & Swing Dance
Martin Luther King Center, 20 Dr. Marcus Wheatland Blvd., 846-4828, 1pm.

Children's Jazz Workshop
Martin Luther King Center, 846-4828, 20 Dr. Marcus Wheatland Blvd., 1pm. Hands-on live musicians program.

Jazz Ferry
RIPTA Newport/Providence ferry location, Perotti Park, America's Cup Ave.

Jazz Train & Wine Tasting
Newport Dinner Train, America's Cup Ave., 841-8700, 6pm. US Navy Jazz Band.

Jazz on the Bay
Bowen's Wharf at Queen Anne Sq., 6pm.

Evening Jazz
OceanCliff Hotel, 65 Ridge Road, 8pm. Features Billy Weston.

Jazz at the Playhouse
Newport Playhouse & Cabaret Restaurant, 102 Connell Hwy., 848-7529. Features Laurel Casey.

Jazz & Blues
Newport Blues Cafe, 286 Thames St., 841-5510, 8pm.

Jazz on the Roof
Hotel Viking roof top, 1 Bellevue Ave., 8pm.

Jazz Week in Newport

243

As it turned out, we did get a few sponsors that helped pay for some performers, but that was all. And we worked hard to get just these few sponsors we had.

But, we continued on with the program anyway and produced 18 free events, including an educational lecture, a U. S. Naval Band free outdoor concert and three performances at the Rhode Island State House in Providence.

We were able to convince Rhode Island's governor to proclaim "Newport Jazz Week." We purchased t-shirts, badges, and buttons.

The program ran reasonably well but we were unable to break even. It cost our new organization most of its limited treasury.

The energy and effort put into the program could not be repeated without the support of major sponsorship which was difficult within the confines of a struggling Rhode Island economy. We just couldn't find the sponsorship needed to continue our ambitious program however, others have taken our ideas and have re-booted the weekly theme. They now call it "Bridge-Fest."

Chapter 68
The 1997 Newport Jazz Festival

Among the Friday evening performances at the International Tennis Hall of Fame's renowned Casino was a tribute to the late Dizzy Gillespie, who had passed away at age seventy-five on January 6, 1993.

The performance that evening featured the horns of Jon Faddis, Nicholas Payton and Clark Terry. It was awesome and I won't easily forget it.

♫ ♫ ♫

Saturday

◆ **Ray Charles.** His troupe once again featured Ray and The Rayettes in full regalia. And as usual, it was the blues at his level. The fans started jumping and cheering. We all began beating and singing along with Ray. It was a great start to this year's festival.

◆ **Dianne Reeves** followed, highlighting mostly African chants and beats. It was different than the Ray Charles presentation for sure. Her rhythm was connected to religion and soul. She has a loyal fan base that was certainly in the house. They appreciated her work more than I did.

◆ **The Nicolas Payton Quintet was next to perform**. Many people think his work resembles Louis Armstrong's from his early days since Nicolas plays the horn like few others do. He has the whole thing -- tone-sweetness, range, tonguing and improvisational talent. He is a trumpet player's trumpet-player. He and his quintet entertained jazz enthusiasts with upbeat numbers that truly belonged at this festival. It was a delight.

◆ **Medeski, Martin and Wood**, a fusion and hip-hop group followed. John Medeski led the quartet at keyboard and piano, with Billy Martin at the drums and Chris Wood on bass guitar. They certainly rattled a few eyeballs, but I had a tough time appreciating their sound and music.

♫ ♫ ♫

Sunday

◆ The great **George Benson** began the day. Wild applause erupted from the crowd from the very beginning. His voice and guitar work was very much at its peak, and he truly entertained the audience.

◆ **Herbie Hancock**'s group featured Herbie at the piano. His music is always labeled "cross-over" from pop to funk. He has his fans and they were here at this performance.

◆ **Wayne Shorter** followed. The saxophone of Wayne Shorter is well known throughout the jazz world. He is also a composer and arranger. His music and energy this day were outstanding as was expected.

◆ **Crisol**. Latin jazz music at its best was to come next, featuring Roy on trumpet, Chucho Valdes from Havana, Cuba on piano, Frank Lacy on trombone and Jose Luis Quintana on timbales. Their music was totally upbeat. We all loved them. The place began rockin' and there was plenty of dancing in the aisles.

◆ **David Sanchez,** Puerto Rico's Grammy Award winning tenor saxophonist followed. He mixed his music with several different rhythms. It was soothing and upbeat. The audience clapped and clapped.

◆ Don Byron's **Bug Music** was to end the performance, featuring Don, a graduate of New England Conservatory in

Boston, on reeds. His music was avant-garde and Klezmer for sure. The bug music was "way-out" to say the least.

Chapter 69
The 1998 Newport Jazz Festival

Saturday

◆ **Aretha Franklin** began the 1998 Newport Jazz Festival. Her demonstrative voice and gospel renditions led the way. She sang blues in an original interpretation, honoring African rhythms. Only Aretha can capture the whole audience with love in her performance. It was effective.

◆ **Chick Corea & Origin** were to follow. Chick's ultra-fusion keyboards combined with the reeds of Anthony Braxton, John Patitucci on bass and Dave Weckl on the drums. Their acoustic sounds were original. The rhythm alone drew the audience's approval.

◆ **Diana Krall's** performance featured more of her voice than her piano playing. Diana had come a long way from her years at Boston's Berklee School of Music. She sang many of her recorded hits with her charming personality right out front. Her fans were in heaven. It was the highlight of the afternoon for many of us.

◆ **Michael Brecker** led his accompanying group that featured Michael on his saxophone throughout their performance. His R&B music didn't connect with me. Still, many applauded his gig.

◆ **The Regina Carter Quintet** was next. The improvisational jazz violinist, cousin to saxophonist great James Carter, played a series of groovy numbers that crossed classical lines into jazz. Her fans were here and they truly applauded her. Many new fans were being developed, including me. It turned out to be an excellent way to end the day. Her skills and new music stayed with us as we left the facilities.

♫ ♫ ♫

Sunday

◆ **David Sanborn** had become the veteran sax player at these Newport concerts. His many fans were here applauding his every sound. He was a great pick to begin today's program.

Burt Jagolinzer

Diana Krall

◆ Performing next was vocalist and composer **Cassandra Wilson**. Her music had brought country, blues and folk into the jazz mainstream. Not everyone thought she belonged here, but her excellent voice attracted me and made me glad she was.

◆ The brassy sounds of **Arturo Sandoval's Hot House Band** immediately captured the audience. Arturo is a Cuban jazz trumpeter, pianist and major composer of Latin-American orchestral numbers. His spectacular trumpet playing solos grabbed us right from the beginning. Wow! Many of us were dancing in the aisles. Arturo took two trumpets, two saxophones, and two trombones together with a piano, drums and bass to resemble an entire orchestra. His creation worked quite well. The music was wonderful.

◆ **Dave Brubeck** and his quartet followed. Dave was on piano, Bill Smith on reeds, with Randy Jones on drums and Eugene Wright at the bass. Their usual famous hits were featured and the audience loved it. So did I.

◆ **Boney James,** a veteran sax player, writer and composer, was known for his blending of Latin and R&B music. He didn't disappoint his many, many fans who came to this concert just for this presentation. The place went wild. He left us asking for more. It proved to be a great ending of the day and weekend.

Chapter 70
The 1999 Newport Jazz Festival

Saturday

◆ **Harry Connick, Jr.** and his band opened the 1999 Newport Jazz Festival. It was Harry's first performance at Newport. He sang, played several instruments and led his accompanying big band. His numbers included a good many of his own well established hits. Harry was certainly at his very best, and we all loved his presentation. It was a great way to start the day and the festival.

◆ Pianist **McCoy Tyner** followed. He was at the peak of his career, as he mixed his music with African rhythms that captured the audience. They applauded. I liked several of their numbers.

◆ **The Hank Jones Trio** came next. Hank, the brother of trumpet-player Thad and drummer Elvin, was a veteran jazz pianist, arranger and composer. He had accompanied many of the great and famous entertainers in music, including a long stint with Ella Fitzgerald. He was joined on stage with noted drummer Jimmy Cobb and fusion double-bassist Eddie Gomez.

◆ **Leroy Jones,** another great trumpet performer from New Orleans, and his quintet, then took to the stage. His group consisted of Don Vappie on banjo, Mitchell Player on bass, Meghan Swartz on piano and John Mahoney on trombone. It was a gasser. They lit up the place.

◆ **The Ned Goold Trio** completed the program. Ned and his blazing tenor saxophone led the group throughout their gig.

♫ ♫ ♫

Sunday

◆ **Will Downing** came next with the reeds of the multi-talented Gerald Albright. Will is a gifted soul singer with R&B influences. Gerald, along with his mighty saxophone playing, also performs on bass guitar, keyboard and vocals. These California talents put on a terrific show and received plenty of applause. It was their first gig at Newport. And it was a good one.

◆ Next was **Keiko Matsui,** the attractive Japanese new-age keyboardist. Her "fusion takes" on original tunes were very different for this festival. Although she had fans here, some of us had a hard time understanding her approach to jazz.

◆ The unique voice of **Kevin Mahogany** ended the show. He captured many of us with his loud and demonstrative romance with the American Songbook. His talent was new to us and we felt his performance that day guaranteed his future success as a premier singer in our world of jazz. We really enjoyed his delivery and beautiful voice. It was a great ending to another Newport festival. We hummed our way home to several of Kevin's tunes.

Chapter 71
A Day and a Half with Harry Connick, Jr.

Festival Productions had hired the Harry Connick Jr. Orchestra to perform at The Casino in Newport on a Friday evening as the opening attraction to the 1999 festival. I was asked to help Harry, his wife and two young children during their stay.

It was an interesting experience. The kids were great. Harry even brought a tutor with him to help with the children's studies. They were easy to have around, and were lots of fun and humorous.

His wife was quiet and reserved, carefully watching over her active children.

Harry told me, "I'm just a member of the band." I quickly responded to that statement, "What do you mean by that remark?"

This gracious Southern gentleman answered, "I might happen to be the leader, the arranger, the soloist, the drummer, the pianist and the lead singer. But I'm just a member of the band."

"Harry, you must mean something else by that answer. What is it?"

"Well, when I'm invited to have dinner with musical people, I say yes, but you must also invite the band. When the hotels offer me a special suite, I say yes but insist they must give suites to the other members of the band, too."

I had the opportunity to talk with several members of his band. They confirmed Harry's unusual treatment and his close and personal association with each member of the musical group.

I found Harry to be very special and unique among entertainers. It was my pleasure to have had the opportunity to have helped him and his young family that weekend.

Chapter 72
The 2000 Newport Jazz Festival

The 2000 Newport Jazz Festival opened with the group Four Play on the Fort Stage, the main stage. It was the beginning of multiple stage presentations at the Fort Adams location.

Producers had decided to create a second stage, and sometimes a third stage, to give more musicians a chance to participate. The change exposed more talent to jazz fans, and allowed new talent to add playing at Newport to their resumes. It was also designed to be a major boost to ticket sales for future events.

On the negative side, many of us, while trying to see some of this new talent, would lose the performances on the main Fort Stage. You had to learn to juggle your schedule to get the most of the program. I'm not sure everyone liked this new concept. It seemed unfair to the elderly, like me, or for the disabled who have problems moving around, who now had to quickly transport themselves to other stages, or miss some of the choice performers.

♫ ♫ ♫

Saturday

◆ The famous fusion-crossover arranger and producer **Bob James** led **Four Play**. His credits include a long stint with songstress Sarah Vaughan. Bob is a veteran keyboardist and was featured in this performance. Joining him on stage was Larry Carlton on guitar, Nathan East at the bass and vocals and Harvey Mason on drums. They were loud and musical. The crowd cheered.

◆ **Dianne Reeves** followed, having returned to Newport for her third appearance. Once again her sound accentuated the bold rhythm of Africa. Her accompaniment featured drums of several types beating their sounds reminiscent of tribal callings. It was clearly a reminder of the core of our art form. She and her group received loud audience appreciation.

◆ **The Carnegie Hall Jazz Band** went on stage next featuring the trumpet of Jon Faddis, who also served as the group's musical director. Joining Jon on many important numbers was the veteran saxophonist Lew Tabackin. The group played terrific arrangements and the solos blended well into the projected melodies. It was a great gig for them and for us.

◆ From Lagos, Nigeria came reedman **Femi Kuti** and **The Positive Force**. Their music was West African by nature and very different. It caught many of us by surprise. Their beat and rhythm were featured prominently throughout the show.

◆ **Kenny Garrett**, bebop saxophonist and flutist, along with his quartet came next. They got the audience going with upbeat numbers. Kenny's versatility was delightful.

◆ Over at the Harbor Stage were the talents of **James Carter** on his saxophone. I unfortunately missed a good amount of his performance while at another stage, but my friends told me he was awesome.

◆ When I returned, I was able to catch **The Deep Banana Blackout** led by Hope Clayburn on saxophone and vocals with their New Orleans style jazz. This funk band from nearby Connecticut was "way-out." Not everyone understood or appreciated their direction or music.

◆ **The Stefon Harris Quartet** came on stage. Stefon was a veteran vibraphonist and marimba entertainer. He was accompanied by Xavier Davis on piano and Tarus Mateen on the drums. Their music was mostly upbeat and we left our seats dancing to their rhythm.

Burt Jagolinzer

♫ ♫ ♫

Sunday

◆ **Cassandra Wilson** took stage. This was her second visit to Newport. Back in 1998, she blended country, blues and folk into her performance. She basically did the same this time and her following applauded her every sound. My friends and I agreed that the blues part of her singing certainly belongs here, but the rest of her music didn't quite fit.

◆ Then came **Celia Cruz,** the aging Cuban music jazz singer. She had been dubbed "Queen of Salsa" and had sung with many great Latin orchestras over the course of her long, spectacular career. And she could *still* sing! Her performance was wonderful and appreciated by all especially by fans of Spanish and Latin jazz -- and there were plenty of them on hand. As always, it was an upbeat gig and she may have stolen the whole show.

◆ **Boney James** was known for taking his tenor saxophone through his unique style of Latin-American interpretation, and blending it with R&B sounds. He did the same in his performance of 1998, but this time he was accompanied by the multi-horns of Rich Braun. The music was totally contemporary. We acted like we understood his music. I'm not sure I did, but it was surely upbeat.

◆ The funk and soul jazz saxophone of **Maceo Parker** came next. He was best known for his work with James Brown in the 1960's. His fans loved every tune. They applauded him with vigor, many of us included.

◆ Saxophonist and composer **John Zorn & Masada** were next. With his klezmer music, he organized religious music and more. Joining him was Dave Douglas on trumpet, Joey Baron on keyboards and Greg Cohen on bass. The music was very interesting and catchy. We applauded.

◆ Over at the Harbor Stage was Karl Denson's **Tiny Universe**. Karl played the sax and flute, with the help of Chris Littlefield on trumpet, Brian Jordan on guitar, David Veith at the keyboard, Chris Stillwell on bass and John Staten at the drums. I was only able to hear and see a portion of their performance, But their fans were there for them. There was a lot of noise and the crowd cheered.

◆ Also on the Harbor Stage was the Juno Award-winning pianist and composer **D. D. Jackson**. Featured with him was guitarist and composer Vernon Reid. I only arrived in time to catch their last number. Their sound was all over-the-place. I couldn't understand what they were trying to accomplish with their music.

◆ Ending the day at the Harbor Stage was **The Black Blade Fellowship**. Their religious theme music was almost preaching. Leading the group were Jon Cowherd on keyboards and Brian Blade on drums. Their music was spiritual and well-received by many.

Chapter 73
Re-Discovering Mike Renzi

Mike Renzi is one of the finest jazz pianists in the world and hails from Providence, Rhode Island. He paid his dues as a youngster by working his way to New York City where his special talents were quickly discovered.

Over his long professional career, he has served and performed with many famous jazz players and the biggest names in show business. The list is impressive and included long stints with Mel Torme, Lena Horne, Jack Jones, Liza Minnelli, Frank Sinatra and Peggy Lee.

Mike is an arranger, composer, soloist, consummate rhythmist, and a walking encyclopedia of the jazz art form. Even today, he is in constant demand as an accompanist for recording studio work. I had followed him since childhood and his early days playing near home.

Recently, he purchased a home in nearby Middletown, Rhode Island, supposedly to begin a formal retirement. Nancy and I have now had the chance to build a new, personal friendship with him.

Mike Renzi

A few years ago, he invited us to New York City. At the time, Mike was music director for the famous long-running children's television program *Sesame Street*. He took us on set, even letting us meet with Big Bird and many of the show's characters.

That day ended with a visit to the infamous Noble Recording Studio, managed by Mike's dear friend and guru Jim Czak. Jim had spent decades working with most of the great artists in the music world. He, like his buddy Mike Renzi, is a veteran pianist as well. While visiting his studio the talented guitarist John Pizzarelli, son of the famous guitarist and entertainer Bucky Pizzarelli, happened to be there.

We spent some private time with them in the recording session and enjoyed this special day.

Mike Renzi is different than most pianists. He doesn't always lean on improvisation when interpreting the composer's works like Erroll Garner, Dave Brubeck or Ahmad Jamal. Instead, Mike reaches for extra ivories that bring out the featured melodies originated by the composer. Few pianists can do that.

He is a confident professional with long years of experience and is a truly model performer. Even now in advancing years, he is playing better than ever.

We are very fortunate to have attended his many local gigs where he continues to highlight his gifted and unique skills through his beautifully defined music.

Most recently, Mike was hand-picked by the great recording star and entertainer, Tony Bennett. Tony was looking for a replacement pianist and Mike just happened to be available.

Today, he travels with Tony, the gifted guitarist Gray Sargent and veteran bassist Marshall Wood. They formally make up the Tony Bennett Quartet.

All of Mike's friends, relatives and fellow performers are proud of Mike. Many speak openly that he deserves the great recognition that he continues to get for his sensational performances.

Chapter 74
The 2001 Newport Jazz Festival

Saturday

◆ **Diana Krall** had recently been elevated to the top of the many jazz polls as the leading female jazz singer in our country, and her performance that day proved it. She was at her best, singing many of her recorded hits and a few new ones. This was a great way to open the festival on the main stage.

◆ Pianist **Dave Brubeck** and his quartet followed with Bill Smith on his alto and other reeds. They performed their famous hits to the delight of the audience. As usual *Take Five* brought all of us to our feet. We loved their performance.

◆ **Karl Denson's Tiny Universe** was next. It was their second appearance, and this time, it would be on the Fort Stage. Karl's saxophone and flute shared the spotlight with Chris Littlefield on trumpet, Dave Veith at the keyboards, John Staten on drums and Chris Stillwell on bass. They produced a lot of noise and the audience cheered.

◆ **The Roy Hargrove Quintet** appeared next. Roy's horn was supported by Jonathan Batiste on piano, Chalmers Alford on guitar, Pino Palladino on bass guitar and Bernard Wright on keyboards. The music sounded more like funk, maybe even edging toward fusion. Roy has a fan base and many were there to applaud him and his group.

◆ **Jerry Gonzalez and The Fort Apache Band** followed. Jerry not only performed on his Latin jazz trumpet but also included his skills at percussion. The music was truly upbeat in the best Latin way. Returning from the other stage I was only privy to their last two numbers, but it appeared that most of the audience enjoyed their sounds.

◆ Meanwhile on the second stage, **Ravi Coltrane**, the son of the late John Coltrane, was performing bebop jazz on his own saxophone. My friends who had stayed there said that his music and group were terrific.

◆ **The Sun Ra Arkestra Group** took to the stage with Marshall Allen. Marshall was a prolific jazz composer, bandleader, piano player and synthesizer performer who led the group. But their eclectic music appeared to be all over the place, and what little I was able to hear left me without a creative understanding of their musical goals. They do have a following, and it was evident in the crowd that supported them.

◆ To the stage came **Big Bill Morganfield**, blues singer and guitarist. Bill is the son of the famous Muddy Waters. His music was light compared to several other groups. Blues enthusiasts were very delighted. There was plenty of clapping.

◆ Ending the day on the second stage was **Nora York,** the daring avant-garde vocalist. I only caught a glimpse of her work, but it was clear that this diva lit up a lot of people -- they stood up and cheered her performance. I feared that I had missed something important.

♫ ♫ ♫

Sunday

◆ **Ray Charles**. His entire organization was here and ready to perform -- and did they ever! It was like a Busby-Berkeley show in Hollywood: there was formal pomp, winded introductions, loud music and arrays of color. Ray was at the piano giving us his best. The Rayettes danced and sang as the backup, and included some solos. The orchestra was excellent with special arrangements and great talented solo work, too. Ray's fans were in heaven, and so were we. It was a happening.

◆ **Natalie Cole** had to follow Ray, and she looked and sounded lovely. Her voice now proved her talent for jazz, though she had totally built her success through other avenues of pop music. Natalie and her people finally pushed her into jazz and to her father's famous tunes. Her new versions of his classic numbers sure pleased us. It was a wonderful performance, and she received the standing applause that she deserved. Her interplay with her dad's original recordings was a first, and we had the honor of enjoying it that day.

◆ **The Wayne Shorter Group** came next. Wayne, a veteran reeds player and composer, had brought some strange modern jazz sounds with him. He was accompanied by pianist Danilo Perez and bassist John Patitucci. Drummer and singer Brian Blade was featured throughout. I had trouble understanding where the music was heading, but their fans loved it.

◆ **Chuck Mangione** had come down from Rochester, New York with his flugelhorn. His magical solos brought down the house and had people singing and dancing in the aisles. Many of the tunes were composed by Chuck himself. He had a huge following that kept cheering throughout his great performance. We couldn't resist clapping with the others.

◆ Chicago's **Kurt Elling Quartet** followed. Kurt, whose established singing voice had developed an excellent following, had many of his people waiting for this performance. They made their presence known. Kurt's music and voice are very different and we enjoyed his presentation.

◆ On another stage, **David Sanchez's Melaza Sextet** began playing. David, from Puerto Rico, is a gifted tenor saxophonist. His works were featured, and he delivered with a Cuban-African Latin classical jazz that captured the audience's attention from the very start.

Performing at the other stage were James "Blood" Ulmer, the free funk and blues acoustical guitarist and vocalist, The Slip, a contemporary avant-rock group from Boston, Uri Caine Trio, featuring Uri, the gifted keyboardist and the Los Hombre's Calientes, featuring Irvin Mayfield on the horn.

It was just *impossible* to see and hear the acts on the other stage. Between a rest-room run, a late lunch, and fighting through the large crowd movements, I was not able to get to the stage when I wanted too. This is just one of the many negatives of these multiple-stage arrangements.

For me and a couple of my friends, the Kurt Elling performance was the final of the day and the weekend. We certainly received our money's worth.

Chapter 75
The 2002 Newport Jazz Festival

Saturday

◆ **Tony Bennett** sang his heart out for the local fans choosing hit after hit from his long, storied career. Then he introduced his talented daughter Antonia Bennett. Antonia had been singing in clubs in Greenwich Village with a Latin band. Not using her father's famous name, his agent happened upon her performance. The agent told Tony about this diva discovery and Tony quickly replied, "That's my daughter!" The agent, after having received the shocking news replied, "We should take her on tour with us!" The rest is history.

Antonia dazzled the surprised audience with a couple of ballads selected from the American Songbook. She and Tony even shared a number together. It was a highlight of the day.

◆ **Cos of Good Music** had to follow. Conducted by the famous comedian Bill Cosby, the group included jazz-rock percussionist Don Alias, Dwayne Burno at the bass, Robin Eubanks on trombone, Ndugu Chancler on drums, Carlos Ward on alto-saxophone and flute, James Williams on piano, Craig Handy on reeds and Jamaaladeen Tacuma on selected percussion. It was an interesting gathering full of musical clash and some funky sounds.

◆ Next was **The Dave Holland Quintet** featured Dave on the bass, with vibraphonist Steve Nelson, saxophonist Chris Potter and drummer Billy Kilson. Their music was well received by the audience.

◆ **Oleta Adams**, spiritual-soul vocalist came to perform. Her songs touched us. Soul singing once again proved that it belongs in our jazz art form, as it was beautifully performed by Oleta.

◆ **The Preservation Hall Jazz Band** from New Orleans took over the stage. Their Dixieland sound was once again heard throughout the park. Featured was an unusual beat from their talented tuba player.

Performing on Other Stages That Day

Once again I was unable to get to the other stage and missed the performances of the Greg Osby Quartet featuring Jason Moran, Ballin the Jack, Sex Mob and Yerba Buena.

♫ ♫ ♫

Sunday

◆ The day began with a performance from the famous songwriter, singer and actor **Isaac Hayes**. His Memphis Soul sound carried throughout Fort Adams. We and the audience were fully entertained by, "the one and only."

◆ Next was the fabulous trumpet of **Arturo Sandoval** and his Cuban jazz style that was totally upbeat. The Latin rhythm got everyone up on their feet. There was dancing and singing throughout. It was a great gig.

◆ **The Nicholas Payton Quintet** appeared next. The New Orleans trained trumpeter was at the top of his career. His sounds, rhythm and jazz presentation was superb. The group was also featuring the reed work of the talented James Carter. It became a wonderful happening.

◆ **Karl Denson's Tiny Universe** performed next. It was a near repeat of their 2000 performance here in Newport. Karl played his sax and flute, with the help of Chris Littlefield on trumpet, Brian Jordan on guitar, David Veith at the keyboard, Chris Stillwell on bass and John Staten at the drums. They produced a lot of noise and their loyal fans were eager to cheer them on.

◆ **Lea DeLaria**, the comedienne and actress, was next to perform. But I skipped it, and instead, I opted to go to the other stage to see Jane Bunnett.

◆ **Jane Burnett**, the Canadian soprano saxophonist and flutist. Jane put on a great performance with her Afro-Cuban jazz melodies. I'm glad I was able to see her gig.

Performing on Other Stages That Day

David S. Ware, Bullfrog featuring Kid Koala, the Antibalas Afrobeat Orchestra and the Holmes Brothers.

Chapter 76
Two Days with Tony Bennett

Back in 1999, Festival Productions contracted with my tour company in Newport to help transport the stars and their families around town during their stay. I was lucky to be personally assigned to Tony Bennett and his daughter, Antonia.

For two and half days, I chauffeured them around Newport giving them whatever they required, and then some.

Tony loved coffee and Antonia was big into Coke and chips.

Neither of them had any money with them. And so, I put out the cash throughout the weekend. Tony does not carry money or credit cards. Wow! I guessed that it was the height of success not to worry about paying for anything. "Just see my agent," he was to say. His agent gladly reimbursed me at the end of the weekend without a problem.

The three of us became close. Tony talked about his thrill at having his own daughter along to sing and supplement his program. This was to be their first major performance together.

It was that Saturday, during his scheduled time on stage, that he delighted the audience when he formally introduced his talented daughter to sing with his group. She was terrific, and local media did a great job reporting about this added surprise.

Tony, who was nearing eighty years-old at the time, was his usual sensation, rekindling the long list of successful numbers that has kept his career in the spotlight.

"I can't believe that I am so busy now, more than any time in my professional life. My son, who is my senior agent, keeps me going all the time," he said. "I should be retired in Florida like my friends… but these young people love me, and I keep performing."

He told me how he got started as a singing waiter in New York. "I was terrible… but a gal in our troupe taught me how to perform. I owe her everything."

He told me his idols were Frank Sinatra and Judy Garland.

Tony called and requested my services for early Sunday morning. Tony came out of the Hyatt-Regency Hotel in shorts with a hat and sunglasses, carrying a suitcase loaded with art supplies.

I took him to the approach of the historic old Trinity Church in downtown Newport. He asked to set up his easel somewhere "out-of-the-way."

And so at the bottom of Church Street by the bushes, we found an excellent spot. I helped him set his easel, chair and supplies facing his chosen subject, this special old church that had been designed by London's famous architect, Sir Christopher Wren, back in 1786.

The day was windy, so he asked if I would hold his easel for him, and I watched as he prepared his oils and canvas. He gave me a lesson not only in preparation but in allowing me to view his skillful techniques. He explained each step to me. It was a unique and valuable session. I even offered to pay him for his personal time. Of course he refused my offer.

He was very grateful to paint the Trinity Church because he was to travel at the end of this weekend, to Los Angeles. Steven Spielberg was sending his private airplane to bring him to a fundraiser where Tony wanted to present Steven with this new painting. Steven had used the Trinity Church and its grounds in the filming of the motion-picture, *Amistad*, a few years prior.

The finished painting was wonderful. He had captured all of the unusual features of this important site. His strokes and techniques well documented his talent.

When we first arrived at this scene it was about 6:30 a.m. No one was around. You could hear a pin drop.

I was dressed with shirt and tie with Tony in shorts and hat. An elderly pair of women began walking through the adjoining open area. They spotted me holding Tony's canvas.

One women said to the other, "Isn't it nice to see a young teacher take the time on an early Sunday morning to teach an older man how to paint?" Tony dropped his brush, took off his sunglasses, looked at me and we both began laughing. I said to Tony, "They should only know."

Tony told that story to many people that day and probably much later.

Chapter 77
The 2003 Newport Jazz Festival

Saturday

◆ Opening the event was the talented songwriter, singer, record producer and musician **India Arie**. With her unusual voice and lyrics she was known for spreading love, healing, peace and joy. For those who listened she did just that. She was very spiritual.

◆ **George Benson followed.** His special voice and guitar playing won over the audience. He sang many of his famous hits. It was a wonderful gig.

◆ **Michel Camilo Trio** began with special guest David Sanchez. Michel who comes from Santo Domingo, is a piano player's piano player and popular composer, and he sure hits those ivories. David Sanchez, from Puerto Rico, accompanied on his tenor saxophone. They performed a Latin and classical style jazz, bordering on new music. Their sound and rhythm caught the attention of the whole festival. We applauded them with vigor.

◆ **The Terence Blanchard Sextet** was next. It sounded as if Terence's trumpet exploded. They performed African-fusion music that had us all beating. It was contagious, and we clapped after each number.

◆ Closing out the Saturday event was **Lizz Wright,** the great gospel and R&B singer and composer. She sang with passion, her message touching on religion and the historical echoes of slavery. Emotions were evident throughout the park. It proved an excellent ending for the day's program.

Performing on Other Stages That Day

Kendrick Oliver and The New Life Jazz Orchestra, Smokey and Miho, and the Vijay Iyer Quartet.

♫ ♫ ♫

Sunday

◆ The opening act was **The Dave Brubeck Quartet.** Bill Smith used his reeds to help them perform their popular hits from both the past and present. The crowd loved every note and tune. It was a great way to begin the day's event.

Burt Jagolinzer

◆ **Cassandra Wilson** went on stage. Having sung here in before, many of us were familiar with her program. Only the blues portion of her music was worthy of my applause, as the rest carried country-western and folk lines. But she did have her followers and they made themselves obvious throughout her gig.

◆ **Stanley Clarke** was next to perform. His bass guitar-swinging compositions crossed funk, soul and rock. It could even be classified as fusion, and he was at his best. A lot of his fans were present. They vigorously applauded.

◆ The talented Puerto Rican, Latin pianist, **Eddie Palmieri,** brought an upbeat rhythm that shook the place. The crowd danced throughout. Latin sound had established its place in the jazz makeup. His performance was dynamite. We all loved it.

Performing on Other Stages That Day

The Dewey Redman Quartet, The Bad Plus, Meshell Ndegeocello, The Detroit Experiment and The Spanish Harlem Orchestra.

Chapter 78
The 2004 Newport Jazz Festival

Saturday

◆ **The Dave Brubeck Quartet** began the day, with Randy Jones on drums, Bobby Militello on alto saxophone and Michael Moore on bass. They lit up the place with Dave's famous hits and standards. Among them was *Take Five*, of course.

◆ **Dianne Reeves** returned once again with Greg Hutchinson on percussions, Peter Martin on piano and Reuben Rogers at the bass. She mixed the American Songbook with an upbeat African-jazz style. She was at her best. Everyone enjoyed her presentation.

◆ **Branford Marsalis** followed. Branford's alto saxophone blended well with guest star, Miguel Zenon on reeds. Also accompanying were Eric Revis at the bass, Jeff Watts on

drums and Joey Calderazzo on piano. Their music was terrific.
Everyone applauded.

Lewis Nash and Burt Jagolinzer

◆ Veteran trumpet player **Jon Faddis** took his turn. The
performance was a tribute to the work of Dizzy Gillespie, Charlie Parker, Benny Goodman and Count Basie. It featured an imposing cast of reigning jazz superstars including Ken Peplowski
on reeds, Clark Terry on horns and some twenty others. It was
quite a sound explosion. Every major instrument was repre-

sented. The rhythm and sound were exceptional. The orchestrations and solos were perfect. We were all standing and clapping throughout their work. It was a highlight of the day.

◆ **Jamie Cullum**, pop singer, songwriter and pianist was next. Accompanying him were Geoff Gascoyne on the bass and Sebastiaan de Krom on drums. I unfortunately missed most of their performance, but the enthusiastic applause indicated their approval. Instead, I attempted to see and hear **The Newport All-Stars** on one of the two other stages. They were a veteran group including the guitar of Howard Alden, James Moody on reeds, Lewis Nash on the drums, with Ken Peplowski on clarinet, Randy Sandke on horn, Cedar Walton at the piano and Peter Washington on bass. It was worth the trouble to get over there.

◆ **Chico Hamilton**, the great jazz drummer, put on a unique solo performance that day. Personally speaking, I need a real melody, but many loved his presentation.

◆ A program titled "**John Coltrane Remembered**," was next. It featured McCoy Tyner at the piano, Michael Brecker on horn, Ravi Coltrane, (John's son) on saxophone, Roy Haynes on drums and Christian McBride on bass. It was truly awesome.

◆ "**Monk's Dream**," featured pianist Barry Harris. Accompanying Barry were Charles Davis on saxophone, Earl May at the bass and Leroy Williams on the drums. Their music was upbeat and the audience loved every sound. We all applauded. Their rhythm and noise were a great ending for the day's events.

Performing on Other Stages That Day

The Ron Carter Trio, with Russell Malone and Mulgrew Miller, Ravi Coltrane Quartet, with Drew Gress, Luis Perdomo and E.J. Strickland, and The Harry Connick, Jr. Quartet with Neal Caine, Charles Goold and Arthur Latin, Lew Tabackin with the Toshi-ko Akiyoshi Trio, featuring Paul Gill and Lewis Nash. Also I missed the third stage, hosted by Marian McPartland with performances by Kenny Drew, Jr., Peter Martin, Mulgrew Miller, Renee Rosnes and Hilton Ruiz.

♫ ♫ ♫

Sunday

♦ **Herbie Hancock** began the day at the keyboard, supported by the veteran Wayne Shorter on saxophone. They were assisted by Dave Holland on bass and Brian Blade on the drums. It was groovy. Herbie was all over the keyboard, as usual. His fans went crazy. Most of the audience were jumping. It was a happening.

♦ **The Ornette Coleman Quartet** was to follow. Ornette led the group with his saxophone. Supporting him was Greg Cohen on the bass, Denardo Coleman, son of Ornette, on drums and Tony Falanga on the bass. Their music was indescribable.

There was very little melody and fusion sounds that were difficult to understand. Yet, he has his many fans and they appreciated the gig.

◆ **The Lincoln Center Jazz Orchestra** under the direction of Wynton Marsalis saluted the work of Duke Ellington, Thelonious Monk and Louis Armstrong. Accompanying Wynton on his horn was vibraphonist Gary Burton, reedman James Carter, jazz violinist Regina Carter and horn players Nicholas Payton and Clark Terry. An amazing fourteen other orchestra members supported the veteran group. They were awesome. The tempo, rhythm and arrangements were right on. It was the highlight of the day for me and my friends. Wow.

◆ **Peter Cincotti,** singer, pianist and songwriter followed. He was assisted by Scott Kreitzer on saxophone, Barak Mori on bass and Mark McLean on the drums. Their music was new to me. I missed some of their beginning work but what I heard and saw was very cool. They had plenty of fans here to applaud.

◆ **The Mingus Big Band** came on next. Participating were Ronnie Cuber on the saxophone, Kenny Drew, Jr. at the piano, Donald Edwards on drums, Wayne Escoffery on tenorsax, Eddie Henderson on trumpet, Conrad Herwig on trombone, Boris Kozlov on bass, Earl McIntyre on tuba, Jeremy Pelt on trumpet, Kenny Rampton on trumpet and Jaleel Shaw on alto saxophone. They played the late Charlie Mingus' original music, much of which he composed himself. I've always had a tough time appreciating and understanding Mingus' music but he had a large following, and many were here to support and hear his work. Certainly they had assembled a terrific group of veteran players to do just that.

◆ **Bill Cosby's** group, **The Cos of Good Music** was to follow. Cosby conducted this collection of musicians himself which included Geri Allen at the piano, Dwayne Burno on the bass, James Carter on reeds, Ndugu Chancler at the drums and Wallace Roney on trumpet. Their upbeat rhythm and sound captured the audience. Most of their work had revolved around bop and fusion and wasn't high on my list of favorites.

◆ Next was **The Jazz Messengers**, with Cedar Walton at the piano, accompanied by Donald Harrison on tenor sax, Bobby Watson on alto-sax, Steve Turre on trombone, Roy Hargrove on horn, Lewis Nash on drums and Peter Washington on the bass. Their music was upbeat and full of alternating solos in full rhythm. It was a great way to end the weekend. I left the event with my ears ringing, full of good jazz and in good spirits.

Performing on Other Stages That Day

The Heath Brothers, Dave Douglas and Vacation Blues, the Lee Konitz Trio, Regina Carter Quintet, Doug Wamble, Geri Allen and The Wallace Roney Duo, Uri Caine, Bill Charlap and Jason Moran.

Chapter 79
The 2005 Newport Jazz Festival

Saturday

◆ **The Wynton Marsalis Septet** began the event. Wynton was at the peak of his career blending beautifully with his chosen accompanists. It was a great way to start the festival.

◆ Double electric bassist **Stanley Clarke** led a trio with Bela Fleck on banjo and veteran French violinist, Jean-Luc Ponty. The music was very different. The banjo work touched a bit on bluegrass. Other sounds crossed both blues and funk. Their fans loved it.

◆ **The Charles Lloyd Quartet** followed, featuring Charles on reeds and flute. He was accompanied by Geri Allen on piano, Reuben Rogers on bass and Eric Harland on the drums. It was upbeat and the solos were excellent. They received a great response.

◆ Singer, composer and pianist **Patricia Barber** took the stage. Her talents produced cabaret music at her best, blending soft original compositions with some standards. Her loyal fans applauded with vigor.

◆ The soulful funk music of **Medeski, Martin and Wood** came next. Their trio was composed of John Medeski on the keyboards, Billy Martin on the drums and Chris Wood on bass-guitar. Though it was not my kind of music, they sure had a fan base. They made a lot of noise.

◆ Trumpet veteran, **Jon Faddis** began performing. His quartet featured Jon and David Hazeltine at the piano, along with Japanese bassist Kiyoshi Kitagawa and Dion Parson at the drums. Special guest was the great trombonist Slide Hampton. They made quality music. It was upbeat with plenty of rhythm. People began beating on their seats. This group closed the day. I walked away with plenty of jazz resonating throughout.

Performing on Other Stages That Day

The Saxophone Summit featuring Dave Liebman, Joe Lovano and Michael Brecker, with Phil Markowitz, Cecil McBee and Billy Hart. I also missed the McCoy Tyner Trio featuring Ravi Coltrane and Terell Stafford, as well as Brad Mehldau, Carla Bley and Lost Chords, T. S. Monk Sextet with Rachael Price, The

Newport All-Stars, the Kurt Rosenwinkel Quartet and the Mark Whitfield Trio.

♪ ♪ ♪

Sunday

◆ **Roy Haynes' Eightieth Birthday Celebration** began the event. Roy, the veteran drummer, was still going strong. His career had spanned some sixty years playing with most of the jazz greats of the past. This special event included the work of Wynton Marsalis on his horn, Chick Corea at the keyboard, Gary Burton on vibes, Joshua Redman on sax, Christian McBride on bass and Roy on the drums. It was a gasser. These guys made some fantastic noise. It was pure jazz heaven.

◆ **The Dave Brubeck Quartet** followed featuring Dave at the piano, accompanied by Bobby Militello on alto, Michael Moore at the bass and Randy Jones on drums. They did their usual gig, playing most of their past hits. And, as always, when it came to *Take Five*, the place went wild. That classic tune had proven to become one of the most important trademarks of the Newport Jazz Festival.

◆ **Steps Ahead** performed next with Michael Brecker on horn, Mike Mainieri on vibes, Mike Stearn on electric guitar, Steve Smith, singer and composer and Richard Bona on the bass. It sounded like fusion or fusion-bebop, it was hard to tell.

But it exploded with bass and rhythm. It appealed to a certain segment of fans.

◆ **The Chick Corea Trio** took over. Chick led the group with his flashy and upbeat keyboards accompanied by Jeff Ballard on the drums and Christian McBride on the bass. They were loud, featuring Chick pretty much on his own. His following was absolutely thrilled.

◆ **The Dave Holland Big Band** had to follow. Dave, a veteran English drummer, led the group that included Robin Eubanks on slide trombone, along with trombonists, Josh Roseman and Jon Arons. Others participating were Taylor Haskins, Duane Eubanks and Alex Sipiagin on horns, Chris Potter, Mark Gross, Alex Sipiagin and Antonio Hart on reeds, Steve Nelson on the vibes and Nate Smith on the drums. They were awesome.

◆ **The Joshua Redman Elastic Band** came next. Joshua was at his best playing classics and standards. He showed us why he is ranked among the top jazz saxophone players in the world. His amazing performance stole the day and the weekend.

Performing on Other Stages That Day

Don Byron Ivey-Divey Trio, Gary Burton's Generations, Joe Lovano group with the Hank Jones Trio, The Cannonball Legacy Band featuring Louis Hayes, Matt Wilson's Arts & Crafts, Bill

'Round Newport

Frisell Trio, Larry Coryell, Russell Malone & Benny Green Duo, and Julian Lage & Taylor Eigsti Duo.

Chapter 80
The 2006 Newport Jazz Festival

Saturday

◆ **George Benson**, opened the 2006 festival. George continued to perform at the top of his career. His voice and instrument captured all of the audience. He is always a great pick to begin a program.

◆ Singer **Al Jarreau** came next. His tunes had now become way-out. He drifted between pop and bebop and anything else he seemed to choose. Yet, his music still possessed a large following that applauded him.

◆ **Arturo Sandoval** was to follow. His trumpet playing hits high notes like few can do. The Latin-Cuban upbeat rhythm gets everyone moving, even in their seats. This group stole the show. Wow!

'Round Newport

◆ **The Robert Glasper Trio** took the stage. Robert is an African-style blues pianist who was supported by a rhythm-section that made plenty of noise. They brought along with them many loyal fans that clapped and clapped.

Performing on Other Stages That Day

The Preservation Hall Jazz Band, The Luciana Souza Brazilian Duos, Raul Midon, Cyrus Chestnut Quartet, Gold Sounds and Marc Ribot on solo guitar.

♫ ♫ ♫

Sunday

◆ **The Dave Brubeck Quartet** began the concert featuring Dave at the piano and Bobby Militello on alto, Michael Moore on bass and Randy Jones on drums. Their usual gig playing included most of their past hits. When it came to *Take Five* the place started shaking. I think many people had come just to hear that composition.

◆ The "*Queen of African Music,*" **Angelique Kidjo**, was about to perform. She sang diverse African tunes, many of which she had composed herself. The rhythm and sound caught the attention of most everyone. Fingers were snapping and hands were clapping throughout her performance.

◆ The pounding style of tap-dancing that appeared next belonged to that of **Savion Glover**. The choreography was talent mixed with acting. It was unusual in the jazz setting but clearly belonged within our art form.

◆ **The Bad Plus** was next. The veteran trio consisted of Ethan Iverson at the piano, Reid Anderson at the bass and Dave King on drums. This group from Minneapolis played upbeat music with cross melodies and sounds reminiscent of another era, and it was well received by a majority of the audience.

Performing on Other Stages That Day

George Wein and the Newport All-Stars, the James Carter Organ Trio, Avishai Cohen Trio, The Marty Ehrlich Quartet and Christian Scott Quartet.

Chapter 81
The Providence Union's Effort in Jazz

Not to be overlooked, it should be noted that the Providence Federation of Musicians Union has continued their effort to help keep jazz alive in Rhode Island.

The organization conducts performances several times throughout the year. The shows regularly occur at the famous old dancehall, Rhodes-on-the-Pawtuxet, located on Broad Street near the Cranston-Providence line.

Most of the local talent work their craft here. The mixers are always excellent. The music is well-worth the nominal entrance fee.

Nancy and I enjoy dancing to the big bands and smaller groupings that perform at these events. This is a great place to meet other jazz fans.

You can contact Al De Andrade at the federation office for a pre-purchase discount.

Chapter 82
The 2007 Newport Jazz Festival

Saturday

◆ **The Branford Marsalis Quartet**, led by Branford's mighty saxophone began the program. They mixed standards with bop and some new sounds. Their rhythm was upbeat and the audience applauded after each number. It was a great opening group for the day's events.

◆ **The Marcus Miller Group** was next. Marcus who can play bass, clarinet, keyboards, saxophone and guitar was in top form. His musical selection, though, was another story. While the music carried beat and rhythm, the melody was hard to find. They still had their fans, however, who clapped throughout.

◆ Pianist **Dave Brubeck** brought his quartet back to Newport as expected. Accompanying Dave were Bobby Militello on alto, Michael Moore on the bass and Randy Jones on the drums. They played some new tunes, but the fans had come to hear the past hits. When *Take Five* was played the place erupted. They cheered throughout the whole gig.

◆ Straight from Belgium, **Zap Mama** (Marie Daulne) came on stage. She sang sometimes in her native French language and then sometimes in English. Her vocal techniques bent toward African pop music. Although it wasn't for me, she had a fan club here to applaud her every tune.

◆ The multi-talented **Bruce Hornsby**, who solos on accordion and piano and sings, was next to perform. He was assisted by Jack DeJohnette on drums and some piano, with Christian McBride on the bass. Their music was mixed with a taste of the standards but the rest was upscale bebop and fusion. Their set drew a lot of attention and applause.

◆ **Joshua Redman**, tenor saxophonist followed. Joshua, whose career seems to be getting better and better, kept everyone happy with his spectacular playing and complete performance. It was truly one of the highlights of the afternoon. It was a terrific way to end the day's events. Redman's performance was worth the price of the ticket alone.

'Round Newport

Performing on Other Stages That Day

Chico Hamilton and Euphoria, the Brubeck Brothers, Monk Legacy Septet, the Kenny Werner Quintet, Gunther Schuller conducting the Mingus Orchestra, the Roswell Rudd Quartet, Abdullah Ibrahim Piano Solo and the Anat Cohen Quartet.

♫ ♫ ♫

Sunday

◆ **B. B. King** was introduced. The production had all the makings of a great Broadway musical and then some. B.B. was at his all-time, show-time best and his renditions of the blues remained sensational. His voice was clear and melodic, the guitar playing was delightful as usual and his complete accompaniment package was highly professional. The audience kept clapping and swaying. It was a great way to begin the Sunday program.

◆ **Reverend Al Green** followed. He had been inducted into the Rock and Roll Hall of Fame in 1995. His voice offered soul a new meaning, and the audience cooled down to pay close attention to the message -- the rhythm and music had become secondary as the religious themes came across right from the start of his gig. There was praying at every level. No one could compare to Al Green and his jazz ministry.

◆ Seventy year-old **Etta James**. The Queen of Soul sang her heart out on blues, rock and soul numbers. She caught the emotions of the audience who immediately took to her presentation. She captured them all. It was a very special happening and everyone loved it. The Roots Band served as her accompaniment. The award winning hip-hop group blended well with the veteran singer's musical program. It proved to be a winner.

◆ **Paquito D'Rivera's PanAmericana Ensemble** came next. Paquito is a Cuban alto saxophonist and clarinetist who leads this upbeat ensemble with Latin jazz. The rhythm and music took center stage at once and carried well throughout the entire gig. It was terrific, and the audience loved every moment of the performance. It was the highlight of the day.

◆ **The Dizzy Gillespie All-Star Big Band** performed calling themselves *Newport '57 Revisited*, featuring Slide Hampton on the trombone. The band included some of the great names that were available for this happening. Among the large list were trumpeter Roy Hargrove, James Moody and Antonio Hart on reeds. They made a lot of noise. Their music selection was excellent and the sounds and rhythm were a perfect fit. The solos were well performed within the arrangements that they used. It proved to be a wonderful ending for this year's events.

'Round Newport

Performing on Other Stages That Day

Luciana Souza and The New Bossa Nova, Jon Faddis' Teranga, The Music of Rahsaan Roland Kirk, Ben Allison Quartet, Portrait of Bill Evans, The Music of Getz and Jobim and the Donald Harrison Quintet.

Chapter 83
Playing Piano at the Tavern on the Green

The Tavern on the Green Restaurant, which opened in 1934, had once been one of the largest grossing restaurants in America.

Famous weddings took place here, as well as many after-theatre parties and celebrations. The Beatles, particularly John Lennon and his family, were regular visitors.

Movie stars and politicians graced their tables. International presence was a daily occurrence. It was truly "the" place to frequent in the great city of New York.

'Round Newport

Although it closed its doors in 2008 after filing for bankruptcy protection, it still remains one of New York City's finest social memories.

In 2007, just a few months before they closed, Nancy and I had the opportunity to lunch in their famous Crystal Room.

While there, I had the most extraordinary experience to play their special white piano in the entrance to this glass-enclosed magnificent park location. And there were several groups of people dining at the time.

I played a couple of numbers and stopped, careful not to make a fool of myself with my limited piano skills.

But it was another unusual accomplishment and a great musical memory for Nancy and me.

Chapter 84
The 2008 Newport Jazz Festival

Saturday

◆ **Aretha Franklin** opened the program. Her demonstrative and emotional voice was perfect for the gospel themes featured in her performance. Although she touched pop and rock and roll, the religious tunes seemed to be her favorites. The audience began humming and stamping, creating a soul-searching effect. It was an unusual beginning for this year's program.

◆ **Chris Botti** and perfect trumpet was introduced. The young, talented horn player chose to come down into the audience to do a tune. Security just happened to randomly pick my significant other, Nancy, and a five year-old girl, for Botti to serenade. It took place right in the middle of the crowd. This proved to be a special and unique moment, and his performance was excellent.

◆ **The Wayne Shorter Quartet** came on stage. Wayne's saxophone was featured during the gig, and his accompanying group blended well with many of Wayne's original compositions. I still can't understand where his music was going, but many of his followers certainly did.

◆ English rock drummer **Dave Holland** led a quartet featuring Cuban pianist Gonzalo Rubalcaba, saxophonist Chris Potter, and percussionist Eric Harland. Their music bordered somewhere between new sounds and funk. Though most of their performance didn't appealed to me; the audience found no problem supporting them.

◆ Double-bassist **Charlie Haden** led a trio made up of pianist Ethan Iverson and guitarist Bill Frisell. The music was straight-ahead, touching some standards yet most of the performance relied on bop and funk. Their fans clapped throughout the gig.

Performing on Other Stages That Day

Lettuce, with Fred Wesley, Melody Gardot, Ledisi, Brian Blade and the Fellowship Band, Jacob Fred Jazz Odyssey, Christian Scott, the Warren Vache Quintet and The Aaron Goldberg Trio.

♫ ♫ ♫

Sunday

◆ Tenor saxophonist **Sonny Rollins** began the day. Sonny was swinging. His accompanying group blended in perfectly with his terrific solos. His music, though favoring African influences, reached into unknown areas of new music. It was tough to follow his musical goals. Many fans came just to hear and see him.

◆ **Herbie Hancock,** the now famous keyboardist and composer had returned to the festival. I found his original works were hard to understand but some of his music did have melodies that were recognizable and we all clapped, honoring his rhythm and upbeat sounds.

◆ **Anthony Hamilton** featured soul-singing with R&B mixes during this set. The religious side of several of the tunes received the audience's attention. It was an unusual gig for most jazz fans.

◆ **The Lionel Loueke Trio** began with Lionel featured on his trusty guitar. His music was well received throughout the performance.

◆ **Soulive**, with trombonist Fred Wesley accompanying, took to the stage. It was soul and then some as the music crossed into funk and other new sounds. The audience seemed to appreciate their work throughout the set.

◆ **The Marco Benevento Trio** was introduced. Marco, who plays piano, organ and keyboards was at his best. Accompanying him was a group featuring the reeds of Chris Potter. Their music was experimental and lacked melody. Yet, there was plenty of support for their style. It was hard for my friends and me to understand the attraction.

Performing on Other Stages That Day

Guillermo Klein and Los Guachos, Chris Potter's Underground, George Wein and his All-Stars, Empirical, Esperanza Spalding and the Mark Rapp Band.

Chapter 85
The 2009 Newport Jazz Festival

◆ **The Dave Brubeck Quartet** opened the program. Veteran alto saxophonist, Bobby Militello, accompanied Dave at his piano. Also in the show were Michael Moore on bass and Randy Jones at the drums. As expected, they performed all their famous hits and as was also expected, when *Take Five* was played, the audience went into frenzy. It was a wonderful way to open the weekend day event.

◆ The charismatic singer and bassist **Esperanza Spalding** followed. Her creative talent was evident right from her first tune. Her style crossed Latin lines that mixed into her own music, and her personality held the audience's attention throughout the gig. We won't forget her performance.

◆ **Brian Blade and the Fellowship Band** took over the stage. Brian led the group with his singing and percussions. Their music was way out, with no signs of a melody that I could hear. But there was plenty of noise, and it kept their fans happy. For some of us, though, we just gazed up at the performance not knowing what to make of it.

◆ **James Carter** and his reeds led a unique organ trio. Leonard King was on drums, with Gerard Gibbs featured on the B-3 organ and keyboards. It was unusual but it blended well into the day's jazz events. James Carter can play anywhere and his solos were terrific.

♫ ♫ ♫

Sunday

◆ **Tony Bennett,** featuring new guitarist, Gray Sargent began the event. Tony, now in his eighties, was again exceptional. He sang mostly his own hits, including *San Francisco* and *Because of You*. His loyal, long-time fans appreciated every tune and applauded after each number. To many it was the highlight of the day.

◆ Tenor saxophonist **Joshua Redman** led an upbeat group that worked hard and sounded sensational. Joshua's solos were wonderful. Many of his fans had waited all day just to hear this set. We were all in jazz heaven.

♦ Veteran drummer **Roy Haynes**, who had played with many of the greatest jazz musicians to ever grace the stage, was still soloing at the top of his career. The music included many of the standards of yesteryear. Older folk, like me, appreciated the selections as well as Roy's talents.

♦ **The Vijay Iyer Trio** was next included Vijay at the piano, and was surrounded by Stephan Crump at the bass and Marcus Gilmore on the drums. Their music was African influenced for the most part, and the rhythm and sound were both religious and soul-searching. They, too, had a large fan base who continued to applaud their performance.

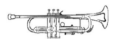

Chapter 86
The 2010 Newport Jazz Festival

Saturday

◆ **Chick Corea's Freedom Band** began today's concert, featuring vocalist Kenny Garrett, the bass of Christian McBride and the drums of Roy Haynes. Chick banged away on his keyboards and blended with the group on a variety of tunes. His movement towards funk and new music was evident from the very beginning of the set. A lot of young people were beating and dancing to the rhythm and music.

◆ Next was **Jamie Cullum,** an English jazz pop singer, composer and pianist. His music seemed off in another direction, however, he had plenty of fans here to cheer him on to victory. But I couldn't get past his first tune.

The Newport Jazz Festival at Fort Adams.

◆ **The Maria Schneider Big Band** took stage. Maria was known as an arranger, composer and big band leader, and she did all of that in her performance here in Newport. The band consisted of quality veteran musicians and they made plenty of big band noise. The place was jumping.

◆ **Ahmad Jamal** appeared next. The great jazz pianist's command of the ivories is quite different than most other veteran pianists. His approach to beautiful standards is light, yet masterfully captures the complete melodies of the composers. His works are very recognizable and quite romantic. The whole gig was absolutely wonderful.

◆ **The Jazz Mafia's Brass, Bows and Beats** was led by Adam Theis on trombone, trumpet, bass, tuba and keyboards, with Joe Bagale on vocals and drums and Karyn Paige singing.

Their music was hip-hop classical. The young fans appreciated their wild gig.

◆ **Anat Cohen**, the Israeli jazz clarinet and saxophone wiz selected a small group of New York City talented musicians to back him up. From Jewish klezmer to funk, their sounds easily penetrated the weekend crowd. They were really upbeat and many of Anat's young followers began screaming and clapping. It was a cool performance.

◆ **The Newport All-Stars** took the stage. Howard Alden led the group with his guitar, and supported by George Wein at the piano, Randy Sandke on trumpet and guitar, and special guest valve-trombonist, Bob Brookmeyer. They led into some great standards with wonderful improvisational solos. It was well received by the audience and proved to be an excellent performance.

◆ **Mark O'Connor's Hot Swing** followed. With his very talented group of specially-picked musicians, Mark played his violin in jazz remembrance of the late Stephane Grappelli who had been Mark's teacher and idol. The violin captured the attention of most of the fans. They found the music very different, but were accepting of the violin as a meaningful instrument within the jazz art form.

◆ **Darcy James Argue's Secret Society** was next. This new-era, big brass band from the swinging Balkans produced experimental music in folk, and art-rock-fusion. It was tough to understand, but it was noisy and upbeat and included plenty of swaying rhythm.

◆ **Fly** followed, featuring Jeff Ballad on his guitar, with Larry Grenadier on double-bass and Mark Turner on reeds. The music was cool. The audience loved it and applauded throughout their performance.

Performing on Other Stages That Day

The J. D. Allen Trio, The Julian Lage Group, Trio Da Paz with Harry Allen, Rez Abbasi's Acoustic Quartet and The Berklee Global Jazz Institute Septet.

♫ ♫ ♫

Sunday

◆ The eclectic works of keyboardist **Herbie Hancock** began the program. He and his group's selections not only reached for new sounds but also included some of his original compositions. The fans loved every note and every tune. They applauded and applauded. Most thought it was a great way to begin the day's concert.

◆ **Chris Botti** and his trumpet performed next. Supported by a select group of jazz veterans, Chris put on a terrific performance. His music encompassed a few standards and some original compositions. His fans screamed for more after he completed his set but to no avail. It was a wonderful presentation.

◆ **Wynton Marsalis** and his trumpet led a group of New Orleans' super musicians. They touched Dixieland, hip-hop, some fusion and a couple of standards. It was as if Wynton reached for the top of his successful career during this performance. He was magnificent. It was a very special set.

Wynton Marsalis

◆ **Arturo O'Farrill and Afro-Latin Jazz Orchestra** opened with upbeat rhythm that brought everyone off their seats swaying and dancing. His loud and pounding sounds kept getting faster and more pronounced. It became modern jazz and swing at its best. Wow! The performance was to steal the afternoon's thunder.

◆ **Amina Figarova**, pianist and composer from Azerbaijan, brought some soul and African music to the event. She displayed her skills at the piano throughout the set and her fans got exactly what they came for. They were loud and let themselves be known.

◆ **Conrad Herwig's Latin Side of Herbie** followed. This band re-arranged Herbie Hancock's original pieces to a Latin style. The results were very different. Herbie's music was still difficult to understand, though the new Latin beat made it more pleasing to the ears. The younger crowd sure appreciated this approach and applauded after each tune.

◆ Horn great **Jon Faddis** closed the weekend. Jon is still at the peak of his brilliant career, performing better than ever.

Performing on Other Stages That Day

Ken Vandermark's Powerhouse Sound, The David Binney Band, Marshall Allen-Matthew Shipp-Joe Morris, Jason Moran Bandwagon, Ben Allison Band, Gretchen Parlato, and The Matt Wilson Quartet.

Chapter 87

Old Musicians Attempt Coming Back

A few years ago I attempted to play my horn again. It had been gathering dust in the storage closet.

Like many former musicians, recalling the memories of previous decades in the performing world will always be precious.

And so, several of my friends thought it might be fun to get together with our old instruments and see what we could salvage.

One of the guys pointed out that actors George Segal and Woody Allen get together in a group each week in New York City and they make darn good music.

Well, we tried, but it didn't work out. One guy got sick, another had business problems and a third's reeds needed overhauling.

Burt Jagolinzer

I had trouble with the basic scales as my most important lip muscles had deteriorated.

The attempt was genuine. We tried our best but it was not to be. Maybe a new plan would surface in the future.

We remain among a long list of frustrated musicians, hoping to someday rekindle a piece of our musical past.

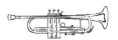

Chapter 88
The 2011 Newport Jazz Festival

Saturday

◆ The talented jazz and classically trained violinist **Regina Carter** and her group called **Reverse Thread began the program. It featured Yacouba Sissoko, the master Kora** player from Mali. The music featured a mixture of jazz instruments and Kora, or African harp and Fula flute. Their melodies and compositions captured an African-Jewish folk style. It was tough to understand, but the instrument sounds were very interesting.

◆ Japanese pianist and fusion composer **Hiromi** performed solo. Her music was billed as post-bop and progressive-rock. She has a following and they applauded her throughout her set.

◆ **Michel Camilo and Mano-Mano followed next.**
Michel was at the piano accompanied by the Latin percussionist, Giovanni Hidalgo, and guitarist John Benitez. They had good rhythm and sound, but the melody was difficult to locate.

◆ **Wynton Marsalis** brought a terrific group of musicians to his set. Wynton was at his usual best and his accompanists blended right along with him. His large legion of fans applauded after each tune. It was a wonderful performance. Most of us loved it.

◆ **Al Di Meola's World Sinfonia** took the stage after Wynton. It was to be the final group on the day. Al, the veteran rock guitarist that he was, performed with the group that featured Gonzalo Rubalcaba, the noted Cuban pianist and composer. Their music was a combination of pop and rock with a Latin touch. They had their fans and the applause continued throughout their gig.

Performing on Other Stages That Day

"Mostly Other People Do The Killing, The New Black Eagle Jazz Band, Eddie Palmieri's Latin Jazz Band, Ambrose Akinmusire, Trombone Shorty & Orleans Avenue, The Joey DeFrancesco Trio, Esperanza Spalding & Friends, Steve Coleman and Five Elements, Randy Weston's African Rhythms Trio and Grace Kelly with Phil Woods.

♫ ♫ ♫

Sunday

◆ **The Mingus Big Band** opened the day. They were loud and made a lot of noise. It was a large group of veteran musicians who came to play some of Charles Mingus' original compositions. The music was strange to me and I just couldn't accept their direction, but it did get the Sunday program going.

◆ Saxophone great **Joshua Redman's James Farm** was introduced. This acoustical jazz quartet was led by Joshua with Aaron Parks on piano, Matt Penman on bass and Eric Harland on the drums.

◆ **Angelique Kidjo** followed. She is a Beninoise singer and songwriter known as the "Queen of African Music." Her sound is a mix of Caribbean Zouk, Congolese rumba and African-pop. She also touches Latin-rock. The sounds are upbeat but the music is difficult to interpret.

◆ **Charles Lloyd's Sangam** came next. Charles performed on reeds, with the Indian Master percussionist Zakir Hussain and Eric Harland on the drums. This group was loud, full of energy, swing and depth. Their fans were delighted.

◆ **Trombone Shorty and Orleans Avenue** took over the stage. Shorty, whose real name is Troy Andrews, not only plays trombone, but also trumpet. Accompanying him were Mike Ballad on the bass, Dan Oestreicher on baritone-saxophone, Tim McFatter on tenor-saxophone, Pete Murano on the guitar and Joey Peebles at the drums. Their music was jazz-funk and rap. They made plenty of sound but the melody was somewhere else.

Performing on Other Stages That Day

The John Hollenbeck Large Ensemble, The Berklee College of Music, Mario Castro Quintet, The Brubeck Brothers Quartet, Miguel Zenon's Puerto Rican's Songbook, Avishai Cohen, Esperanza Spalding, The Ravi Coltrane Quartet, Apex: Rudresh Nahanthappa and Bunky Green and Steve Coleman, Ravi Coltrane and Miguel Zenon.

Chapter 89
The 2012 Newport Jazz Festival

Saturday

◆ The Grand Master drummer **Jack DeJohnette** opened the day's events. His talent gives percussion a new meaning as he dazzles the drum world with his energy and rhythm. His fans applauded his set to the very end.

◆ The Cuban **Pedrito Martinez.** Led by his Latin percussion that continued into pop and rock. The rhythm and sound attracted the audience. They cheered after each tune.

◆ **John Ellis and Double Wide.** John with his mighty saxophone led the group which had arrived from their home in New Orleans. Their music crossed into funk and bebop. Most people liked what they saw and heard.

NPR Record Fan Giveaway

◆ **Pat Metheny's Unity Band** was introduced. Pat wielded his guitar into contemporary jazz and post-bop music. With his supporting group they featured some Latin-jazz mixed with fusion. The melody was faint and difficult to understand.

◆ **Three Clarinets** then took over the stage. Veterans Ken Peplowski, Evan Christopher and Anat Cohen stole the show. Their individual solos were terrific. The music crossed from the American standards into some new-music and then some. But their set seemed too short. I had never heard three clarinets play together like this. Everyone wanted more.

◆ **Bill Frisell** and his group then played *"The John Lennon Songbook."* Bill, who is a contemporary jazz guitarist, reached into the music of The Beatles, playing many original compositions written by Lennon. Their fans responded with applause and rightfully so. It was a great set.

◆ **Dianne Reeves**. Her loud and dramatic voice focused on African-American tunes, and her rhythm brought out the drums direct from Africa. She elected to go past the American Songbook compositions that had helped make her successful career. The gig was upbeat and musical.

Performing on Other Stages That Day

The James Carter Organ Trio, Darcy James Argue's Secret Society, Christian McBride's Inside Straight, The Dafnis Prieto Sextet,

Joe Lovano and The Dave Douglas Quintet and Luisito Quintero.

♫ ♫ ♫

Sunday

◆ **Jason Moran and the Bandwagon** opened the program. Jason, a veteran jazz pianist and composer, worked with Nasheet Waits at the drums and Tarus Mateen on the bass. Their music was well received by everyone. It was one of the best performances of the day.

◆ **Vince Giordano & the Nighthawks** followed. Vince and his big band featured music from the 1920's, 1930's, and 1940's leaning on the American Songbook for many pop and romantic standards. The melodies were wonderful and appreciated by most of the audience.

◆ **The Lewis Nash Quintet: Feat** was next on stage. It featured Jeremy Pelt on trumpet, Jimmy Greene on the saxophone and Lewis himself on the drums. The music faded towards funk and bop, and showed they were quality musicians at their best.

◆ **Tedeschi Trucks Band** was next. Derek Trucks and Susan Tedeschi, from Jacksonville, Florida performed blues and rock during their special set. They sure had their fans.

◆ **The Maria Schneider Big Band Orchestra** performed next. Maria, who was a noted composer and band leader, fronted the group. They played arrangements from the old band era and performed them with perfection. The audience received the music and the solos with great applause.

◆ **The Three Cohens came next.** Yuval Cohen played soprano-saxophone, Anat Cohen, clarinet and tenor and Avishai Cohen on the trumpet. They were awesome and captured the day. We appreciated their work and clapped accordingly.

Performing on Other Stages That Day

Ryan Truesdell's Gil Evans Centennial Project, Kurt Elling, Rudresh Mahanthappa, The Berklee Global Jazz Institute Sextet, Jenny Scheinman and Bill Frisell, The Ambrose Akinmusire Quartet, John Hollenbeck, Gretchen Parlato & Lionel Loueke.

Chapter 90
A Jazz Find in Canada

While on a trip to Montreal just this past year, Nancy and I happened upon a jazz club, The House of Jazz, on Aylmer Street in the heart of downtown Montreal.

There, we discovered the piano talents of Taurey Butler. Performing with a trio in his three-nights a week regular gig, he entertains patrons with gifted touches on the keyboard like few can do.

While talking with him during a break, he mentioned that his mentor has always been the late piano titan, Oscar Peterson, whom he had met and idealized. Taurey's work documents his determination to play like Peterson.

Yet much of his technique reminded me of other piano masters, including Errol Garner and Fats Waller. You can also detect a little of the great Teddy Wilson in his work.

He hits the keys with confidence, excitement and gusto. The tunes are performed with melodic recognition joined by upbeat improvisations that are truly his own.

We purchased his latest CD and play it regularly.

Taurey is a talent not yet fully discovered. His wonderful work is a must for jazz enthusiasts visiting the Montreal area.

Chapter 91
The 2013 Newport Jazz Festival

Saturday

◆ A fabulous group from Boston's **Berklee College of Music** began the next day. Their arrangements and musical presentations were highly professional and well received by the arriving crowd. It proved to be a great way to start this afternoon event.

◆ **The Michel Camilo Sextet**. Michel's dazzling piano-playing was featured throughout, though his melodies stretch far into never-never land. Most of the music was original compositions. However, his piano talents outweighed the strangeness of his musical direction. We loved his performance.

◆ Veteran keyboardist **Herbie Hancock** joined **The Wayne Shorter Quartet**. The focus of this year's performance was the celebration of Wayne's eightieth birthday. Wayne is even more popular today than he was several decades ago, and he still writes and arranges new music. Blending with Herbie, the quartet produced sounds and rhythms difficult to follow and understand. However their fans still applauded at every turn.

◆ **Esperanza Spalding Radio Music Society** was next. Esperanza's creative talent as a singer-bassist was put to the test immediately as she crossed Latin musical lines into her own mixed sounds. Her charismatic singing kept the audience's attention throughout her gig. This performance is hard to forget.

◆ **The Marcus Miller Group** followed. Marcus played an electric bass that complemented his talented musical accompaniment bordering on rock-fusion. His loyal fans loved his work and applauded vigorously, but it just wasn't my kind of music.

Performing on Other Stages That Day

The Mary Halvorson Quintet, the RIMEA Senior All-State Jazz Band, Amir Elsaffar, Ray Anderson The Pocket Brass Band, The Bill Charlap Trio, The Robert Glasper Experiment, The Rez Abbasi Trio and Terrence Blanchard.

♪ ♪ ♪

Sunday

◆ **The University of Rhode Island Jazz Festival Big Band** opened things up. With two alternating directors they blew the place out. These young musicians were a fresh new talent for jazz. Their solos were so professional, exhibiting improvisations like that of veterans, and the performance featured master arrangements. Everyone got to their feet and clapped following each number.

◆ **The Joshua Redman Quartet** followed. Joshua was once again at his very best emotionally blasting away on his tenor saxophone and we, as critics, found no cause to complain. He received more attention and applause than any other performer at the day's events.

◆ **Chick Corea and The Vigil** came next. Chick, with his famous keyboards, played fusion and beyond fusion with his group. Many of his fan base stood up and cheered for his unusual performance, as he improvised with each of his band members, as well as for his many famous hits.

◆ **Eddie Palmieri's Salsa Orchestra** took to the stage. His Pan-American ensemble featured Eddie on alto saxophone and clarinet playing Latin jazz. Everyone danced in the aisles. I danced along with them -- it was totally contagious. This set stole the show in both performance and music.

◆ **The Dizzy Gillespie Big Band** was introduced, under the direction of Paquito D'Rivera. The silky smooth tone from his alto-saxophone and his other reeds helps him stand apart from other veteran performers. Together, with the other members of the big band, they played many of the successful hits that Dizzy had touched. It was upbeat and the music was a joy. It was a great way to end the day and weekend event.

Performing on Other Stages That Day

The Donny McCaslin Group, The Massachusetts All-Star Jazz Band, Jim Hall, Jon Batiste and Stay Human, Dee Alexander, The Dirty Dozen Brass Band, Hiromi, The Trio Project, The Steve Coleman Projects, Roy Haynes' Fountain of Youth Band and David Gilmore and Numerology.

Chapter 92
Today and the Future of Jazz

Today's jazz focus is written and performed around fusion, be-bop, Latin and new music.

African rhythms are regularly included and played within the mainstream, including soul and religious themes. Dixieland will always be a part. The big band, though having a limited market today, will hopefully continue on as well.

Unfortunately, few American standards are considered today when planning or performing a gig. The current generation seeks newer combinations instead of the older compositions for the maximum movement and rhythms that they bring. And the festival talent selection committees are choosing these favorites accordingly.

Jazz has a great future with young students receiving better formal musical education today than in the past. Their chances to play festivals and other events have broadened. A jazz musician's life today is a major improvement over where it had been decades ago.

The popularity of jazz as an art form should keep growing, offering new joy and happiness to its audience and listeners around the world.

Chapter 93
Passing the Torch

When older enthusiasts like George Wein, others and I run out of steam for the art form, the reins must be passed to a new class of experienced veterans who can carry, protect and advance jazz, it's reputation, culture, history and balance in the contemporary music world.

Foremost in that line might be Wynton Marsalis, who by himself has elevated the work examples of a jazz performer, not only with his serious education and manners, but with his appearance (always with white shirt, tie and suit, not sport clothes or sport jacket.) He represents jazz in both performance and in perfection.

How lucky we jazz fans are to have had his rise into our music leadership within the last couple of decades.

His brother Branford, Harry Connick,Jr. and a short list of others will no doubt join Wynton to help the industry survive.

George Wein's successors, Festival Productions, and his foundation, will hopefully maintain their wonderful stage opportunities for the new talent and for acclaimed performers.

With this in place, jazz should be safe for many decades to come.

Long live our music.

Appendix I
The So-Called Nick-Names

Many of the great performers had nick-names. See how many you can identify.

Name All= *Brilliant*, Minus One=*Excellent*, Minus Two=*Very Good*, Minus Three=*Good*, Others=*Time for Research*.

Zoot, The Hawk, Dizz, Count, Hamp, Duke, Sassy, Mr. Five by Five, Louie, Fatha, Satchmo, Red, Woody, Hoagy, Velvet-Fog, Bird, Carmen, Monk, Buddy, Benny, Oscar, Bing, Natalie, Sonny, Ramsey, Aretha, Mahalia, Ella, Prez, The Train, Sweets, Peanuts, Chet, Cannonball, Wild Bill, Marion, Monty, Getz, Lionel, Maynard, Milt, Teddy, Max, Toots, Slide, Dexter, Vic, TD, Frank, Sarah, Peaches.

Appendix II
The Author's Choice

Here are my personal opinions on the finest musicians in each performance category:

<u>Singer Female Jazz</u>
1. Ella Fitzgerald
2. Sarah Vaughan
3. Carmen McRae

<u>Male Jazz Singer</u>
1. Mel Torme
2. Joe Williams
3. Mark Murphy

Burt Jagolinzer

Jazz Pianist
1. Oscar Peterson
2. Dave McKenna
3. Teddy Wilson
4. Monty Alexander

Jazz Bassist
1. Milt Hinton
2. Jay Lenheart
3. Charlie Mingus

Jazz Drummer
1. Gene Krupa
2. Buddy Rich
3. Max Roach

Jazz Trumpet
1. Maynard Ferguson
2. Bobby Hackett
3. Dizzy Gillespie

Jazz Flugel
1. Chris Botti
2. Clark Terry
3. Jon Faddis

Bari Saxophone
1. Gerry Mulligan

'Round Newport

Tenor Saxophone
1. Lester Young
2. Dexter Gordon
3. Scott Hamilton

Alto Saxophone
1. Charlie Parker
2. Stan Getz
3. Paul Desmond

Clarinet
1. Benny Goodman
2. Artie Shaw
3. Ken Peplowski

Vibes
1. Lionel Hampton
2. Terry Gibbs

Harmonica
1. Toots Thielemans
2. Mike Turk

Jazz Saw
1. Irving Lipson
2. Ed Bosko

Burt Jagolinzer

Trombone
1. Slide Hampton
2. Al Grey

Guitar
1. Wes Montgomery
2. George Benson
3. Herb Ellis

Jazz Band
1. Count Basie
2. Duke Ellington
3. Benny Goodman

Jazz Band Leader
1. Duke Ellington
2. Stan Kenton
3. Woody Herman

Jazz Entertainer:
1. Louis Armstrong
2. Duke Ellington
3. Cab Callaway

Blues Performers
1. Ray Charles
2. B .B .King
3. Billie Holiday
4. Joe Williams

<u>Best Jazz Performances</u>
1. Benny Goodman at Carnegie Hall
2. Duke Ellington's 1956 Newport
3. Jam Session at First Newport Festival

'ROUND NEWPORT

words and music by Burt Jagolinzer ©2014

Thelonious didn't write it, as you will hear
This little ditty will make it very clear 'Round Newport

There's rhythm and song, and you'll know you belong
'Round Newport

Dancin' and prancin' and not out of sight, Come visit this city by day
or by night 'Round Newport

You'll find Chowda and Jazz, and a lot of pizazz 'Round Newport

On Spring Street and Thames and America's Cup too, You'll shop
craft and goodies for me and for you 'Round Newport

This island is known for its soft Summer Breeze, And its jazz in the
evening that'll put you at ease 'Round Newport

The Atlantic Ocean, where sea is king, You'll find beaches and jazz,
more than anything 'Round Newport

The water is cool, by the beach, near the sand, For swimming and
clamming, and one heck of a tan 'Round Newport

It's Rhode Island's resort, and a must to see, With jazz in the evening
that's attractive to me 'Round Newport

'Round Newport

There's sailing and tennis, first class you will note,
mansions and museums and many a boat 'Round Newport

When leaving old Newport and heading to home,
You'll know you vacationed and not alone

You'll have seafood aroma... and sand in your shoes
As you leave our island and heading toward home

At First Beach you'll swim with a medium tide
Where a child on carousel will have a good ride 'Round Newport

You'll find surfers at Second, with big vibrant waves
Floating on sea water, in a healthy cascade 'Round Newport

Down Third Beach we hustle to private calm water
To bathe with local families, their son and their daughter 'Round
Newport

At night in the pubs you'll find many new visitors
Who will share music and jazz with any inquisitor 'Round Newport

Finally, and so, when preparing to go
With tears in your eyes, you've wanted to know
Why Newport is special with all of its glitter
It's the place to come and see, even with a baby-sitter 'Round Newport

Now pass on the word to your friends and your mother
And come back soon, to toast our great summer 'Round Newport

Acknowledgements

The author would like to gratefully acknowledge:

- Steven and Dawn Porter, at Stillwater River Publications.
- Attorney, Barbara Slater, for her encouragement.
- Kenneth Jagolinzer, for his praise and initial proof reading.
- Carol Gates, for her master proof reading and expertise.
- Nancy Parenti, my significant other, for her continual encouragement and patience.
- And, Almighty God, who in his infinite way has made all this possible.

Photo Credits

Front Cover: "Miles Davis Returns to Newport" Circa 1985, © Burt Jagolinzer, modified from original with permission.

Chapter 3: "First Newport Jazz Festival Program" 1954, Festival Productions, New York, NY, from the collection of Burt Jagolinzer.

Chapter 3: "Pee Wee Russell Publicity Still," from the collection of Burt Jagolinzer.

Chapter 5: "Newport Jazz Festival Program," 1955, Festival Productions, New York, NY, from the collection of Burt Jagolinzer.

Chapter 5: "The Downbeats" 1958, Taken at the Polish-American Club, Valley Falls, RI, © Burt Jagolinzer.

Chapter 6: "Three Guys From Providence" April, 1995, Scottsdale, AZ © Burt Jagolinzer,"Rhode Island Jazz Singer to Put on Show on Island," 2000, *Newport Daily News.*

Chapter 7: "George Wein Hall of Fame Certificate," © Newport Jazz Association.

Burt Jagolinzer

Chapter 8: "Count Basie" Taken at The Aquarium Jazz Club, New York, NY, circa 1946-1948. William P. Gottleib Collection, Library of Congress (Digital ID gottleib.00471). This work is in the public domain.

Chapter 9: "Anita O'Day 1958 Newport Jazz Festival," by Michael Williams. This file is licensed under the Creative Commons Attribution 2.0 Generic license.

Chapter 12: "Louis Armstrong and Willis Conover, Newport Jazz Festival, 1958," by Michael Williams. This file is licensed under the Creative Commons Attribution 2.0 Generic License.

Chapter 17: "Dave Brubeck & Paul Desmond," by Carl Van Vechten, October 8, 1954. Library of Congress (Reproduction Number van.5a51762.) This image is in the public domain.

Chapter 23: "Jazz Musician Duke Ellington," author unknown, November 3, 1954. http://www.defenseimagery.mil;VIRIN:HA-SN-99-00410 (cropped).

Chapter 28: "Ted Casher" © Burt Jagolinzer.

Chapter 36: "Byron Stripling" © Burt Jagolinzer.

Chapter 43: "Bob Wilber" © Burt Jagolinzer.

Chapter 44:.."Chick Corea at Newport Jazz Festival 2010," by Lee Wright, This file is licensed under the Creative Commons Attribution 2.0 Generic license.

Chapter 45: "1983 Kool Jazz Festival Program," 1983, Festival Productions, New York, NY, from the collection of Burt Jagolinzer.

Chapter 47: "JVC Newport Jazz Festival Sign" 1984 © Burt Jagolinzer.

Chapter 49:.."Miles Davis Returns to Newport" Circa 1985, © Burt Jagolinzer.

Chapter 51: "Gerry Mulligan," circa 1980's, by William P. Gottleib. William P. Gottleib Collection, Library of Congress (Digital ID gottleib.16211). This work is in the public domain.

Chapter 58: "Frank Weiss of the Count Basie Orchestra," © Burt Jagolinzer.

Chapter 65: "Burt Jagolinzer and George Wein," Taken at The Newport Casino, 1995, © Burt Jagolinzer.

Chapter 67: "Jazz Week in Newport," 1996, *Newport This Week.*

Chapter 69: "Diana Krall at Newport" 1998, © Burt Jagolinzer.

Chapter 73: "Mike Renzi," circa 2009, by anonymous. This photo is in the public domain in accordance with the terms of the Free Art License 1.3.

Chapter 78: "Lewis Nash & Burt Jagolinzer," © Burt Jagolinzer.

Chapter 86: "Newport Jazz Festival 2010," by Lee Wright, This file is licensed under the Creative Commons Attribution 2.0 Generic license.

Chapter 86: "Wynton Marsalis at the Oskar Schindler Performing Arts Center," by Eric Delmar. September 13, 2009. This work has been released into the public domain by its author.

Chapter 89: "NPR Record Fan Giveaway," from the collection of Burt Jagolinzer.

Acknowledgments: "Newport Jazz Festival Program Collage," 2014, Taken by Steven R. Porter, © Stillwater River Publications.

Back Cover: "Burt Jagolinzer" 2014, Taken by Steven R. Porter, © Stillwater River Publications."Eighties Festival Crowd with Burt & Ken"© Burt Jagolinzer.

Made in the USA
Charleston, SC
03 November 2015